# THE 50 GREATEST FASHION DESIGNERS

THE PEOPLE WHO HAVE STYLED OUR CLOTHES

# THE 50 GREATEST FASHION DESIGNERS

THE PEOPLE WHO HAVE STYLED OUR CLOTHES

EMMA BAXTER-WRIGHT

SIRIUS

SIRIUS

This edition published in 2025 by Sirius Publishing, a division of
Arcturus Publishing Limited,
26/27 Bickels Yard, 151–153 Bermondsey Street,
London SE1 3HA

Copyright © Arcturus Holdings Limited

All rights reserved. No part of this publication may be reproduced, stored in a retrieval system, or transmitted, in any form or by any means, electronic, mechanical, photocopying, recording or otherwise, without prior written permission in accordance with the provisions of the Copyright Act 1956 (as amended). Any person or persons who do any unauthorised act in relation to this publication may be liable to criminal prosecution and civil claims for damages.

ISBN: 978-1-3988-4450-6
AD011635UK

Printed in China

# CONTENTS

INTRODUCTION ............6

CHARLES FREDERICK WORTH ...........8

JEANNE LANVIN ...............12

PAUL POIRET ................16

JEAN PATOU ................20

CHARLES JAMES ...............24

GABRIELLE CHANEL ...............28

MADAME GRÈS ...............32

ELSA SCHIAPARELLI ...............36

CRISTÓBAL BALENCIAGA ...............40

CHRISTIAN DIOR ...............44

HUBERT DE GIVENCHY ...............48

CLAIRE McCARDELL ...............52

PIERRE CARDIN ...............56

OSSIE CLARK ...............60

MARY QUANT ...............64

PACO RABANNE ...............68

YVES SAINT LAURENT ...............72

HALSTON ...............76

KENZŌ TAKADA ...............80

VALENTINO GARAVANI ...............84

YOHJI YAMAMOTO ...............88

STEPHEN SPROUSE ...............92

KATHARINE HAMNETT ...............96

FRANCO MOSCHINO ...............100

THIERRY MUGLER ...............104

DONNA KARAN ...............108

ISSEY MIYAKE ...............112

VIVIENNE WESTWOOD ...............116

PAUL SMITH ...............120

REI KAWAKUBO ...............124

JEAN PAUL GAULTIER ...............128

CALVIN KLEIN ...............132

GIORGIO ARMANI ...............136

CHRISTIAN LACROIX ...............140

MARTIN MARGIELA ...............144

AZZEDINE ALAÏA ...............148

JIL SANDER ...............152

GIANNI VERSACE ...............156

KARL LAGERFELD ...............160

TOM FORD ...............164

DOLCE & GABBANA ...............168

DAPPER DAN ...............172

JOHN GALLIANO ...............176

ALEXANDER McQUEEN ...............180

MIUCCIA PRADA ...............184

DRIES VAN NOTEN ...............188

MARC JACOBS ...............192

IRIS VAN HERPEN ...............196

PHOEBE PHILO ...............200

RICHARD QUINN ...............204

INDEX ...............208

# INTRODUCTION

The language of fashion is complex, unashamedly superior to the basic necessity of simply dressing; it takes its cues from the shifting moods of culture, presents humour through rebellious provocation, and playfully embraces radical concepts in order to confuse the consumer. Influenced by an ever-changing society that spins increasingly faster, fashion in all its challenging guises has an inescapable impact on the way we present our own image to the world, boosting confidence and creating beauty as it touches everyone in different ways.

In the late 1960s, Gabrielle Chanel (perhaps the most famous designer ever) articulated the inclusive nature of this ephemeral art form, succinctly telling a journalist, 'Fashion is not something that exists in dresses only. Fashion is in the sky, in the street; fashion has to do with ideas, the way we live, what is happening.'

The game has changed; the principles have not.

Fashion as the exclusive domain of the wealthy woman, with the dictates 'of repressive silhouettes and impractical hemlines', no longer exists. Today, the exploratory atmosphere is more democratic, more accepting of difference. The frenetic search for ways to express individuality through clothing are numerous and, thankfully, the existence of one definitive look as decreed by a feted designer has long been redundant. Profound changes have reshaped fashion over a 150-year period; the grand haute couture designers of old, who were once considered tradespeople, have morphed into increasingly famous celebrity figures required to act as the commercial face of the label they represent.

With several large conglomerates owning many of the iconic brands associated with luxury, the business of fashion equates to colossal sums of money; but it is still the individual genius of the designer, with their own artistic vision, that shapes direction and success.

This book highlights 50 designers whose indisputable talent in interpreting the world they occupied has made them worthy of inclusion; creative men and women who have broken down social taboos, liberated the female form, taken inspiration from modern art and anarchic street culture, and championed anti-fashion aesthetics that explore boundaries of distortion in relation to the human body. For many, the unique ideas they generated have become synonymous with their name and a specific period in social history. Now, thanks to the relentless speed of a commercial market that greedily devours innovation, it may be harder for a designer to stamp such an indelible footprint on their *oeuvre*. Facilitated by the global accessibility of the internet, fashion by its nature is fleeting, sometimes obsessed with a preoccupation for novelty and shock tactics, but further examination of the 50 greatest designers reveals their depth of interest with the artisan elements of their profession – the importance of traditional craftsmanship, complex methods of cutting and draping fabric that result in unadulterated simplicity, and the invention of modern synthetics that clone and supersede the luxurious qualities of natural fabrics. Most of the designers featured are household names, others perhaps are less well-known, but all of them have played a significant role in the evolution of fashion history. For the individual who celebrates and appreciates the crazy antics and provocations, handed down in a continuous lurex thread from one generation to the next, these designers who dazzle us with their avant-garde concepts can only ever be described as fashion gods.

INTRODUCTION

**LEFT:** The 'Face' dress by Yves Saint Laurent was part of a series designed in homage to American Pop Art artist Tom Wesselman shown as part of his Autumn/Winter 1966 collection.

# CHARLES FREDERICK WORTH

**LINCOLNSHIRE, ENGLAND** 1825–1895

**HIGHLIGHTS**
Machine-made lace, haute couture salon with live models to showcase his creations, initiated mass-production techniques.

**DESIGN ETHOS**
Elegance revered as an artistic art form with a nod to practicality.

AS AN ENGLISHMAN WHO DOMINATED THE ELITE AMBIANCE OF PARISIAN HIGH FASHION IN THE 19TH CENTURY, DESIGNER CHARLES FREDERICK WORTH IS OFTEN REFERRED TO AS THE FIRST AND GREATEST COUTURIER.

Supported by the powerful Chambre Syndicale de la Couture, which was founded in 1868, he established a long-standing business, dressing grand society on both sides of the Atlantic as well as many members of European royalty. Appropriate attire consisted of extravagant ostentation, but his decorative embellishment and voluminous use of luxurious fabrics outshone all competitors, bringing him worldwide fame and success. A relentless innovator with experimental ideas that reflected the changing times, he was the first couturier to insist on using live models, including his wife Marie, instead of dressing up a static mannequin, as was the tradition. This reformative process – which encouraged clients to visit his salon to be shown new outfits worn on models, which they could then order to their personal specifications – is considered to be the origin of haute couture dressing.

Despite a reputation for excessive opulence, his elegant creativity also extended to practical considerations for women. He shortened the length of their clothes to allow greater freedom for walking, created comfortable one-piece dresses rather than the accepted skirt-and-bodice combination, and abolished the dangerously cumbersome hoops of the crinoline, redirecting the focus of attention on to a decorative train and later the bustle.

As a 12-year-old child, Worth started his working life in Swan & Edgars – a conventional haberdashery

**ABOVE:** Charles Frederick Worth, the father of modern haute couture.

# CHARLES FREDERICK WORTH

**LEFT:** Silk evening dress, with decorative gold bands on the skirt and bodice, circa the mid-1880s. The flat-fronted style with emphasis on the bustle was an innovation based on practicality, allowing greater freedom of movement than a full hooped crinoline.

**BELOW:** Portrait of the Empress Eugenie, born to Spanish nobility and married to Napoleon III. Her lavish gown created from swathes of heavy satin was typical of Worth in this period. Oil on canvas portrait by Franz Xavier Winterhalter, circa 1854.

shop in London – where he sold dressmaking fabrics and shawls to customers. At 18, he arrived in Paris penniless, but secured employment selling accessories and fabrics at Maison Gagelin, where he met sales assistant Marie Augustine Vernet, who would become his future wife and house model, dressing in Worth's early designs. Her clothes attracted compliments, which led to the owners of the shop allocating Charles a small floor space to sell his womenswear. By 1858, the idea of progressing his own range of clothes seemed viable and he went into partnership with a Swedish businessman called Otto Bobergh, opening a dressmaking shop – Worth and Bobergh – before becoming sole proprietor and establishing the House of Worth in 1870.

Success came quickly. His designs were lavish and expensive but aristocratic society demanded new dresses for every occasion and it was Worth, the most magnificent couturier in Paris, who reaped the financial benefits. His workmanship was meticulous, using 17 pieces of material in a bodice to ensure a comfortable fit, and skilfully employing metres of silk to flatter each individual customer with his bespoke evening gowns. The patronage of Empress Eugénie, consort of Napoleon III, Sarah Bernhardt, Nellie Melba and Lillie Langtry boosted his fame, and dresses were ordered throughout Europe, sight unseen, because of his unrivalled reputation.

He instigated new trends anticipating changes in society, dramatically abolishing the hooped crinoline and replacing it with the Princess line that was cut in one piece, with a narrower silhouette that allowed women greater freedom of movement. Later, focus shifted on to more streamlined shapes that helped redefine the female form, redirecting attention on to the bustle at the back of the dress. An early adopter of technical advancements, he used machine-made lace for trimmings, and industrial dyes to ensure colour co-ordinated shades for the hats, gloves and parasols clients needed to complete their fashionable look. Worth's vision for a global fashion industry was prescient; on his death, his two sons Gaston and Jean Philippe took over the business, which survived for four generations.

# CHARLES FREDERICK WORTH

**OPPOSITE TOP:** Worth's garment label showing immaculate stitching inside the dress.

**OPPOSITE BELOW:** A heavy brocade gown made from cream silk decorated with pink floral sprays all over, c. 1897.

**RIGHT:** Worth was famed for his appreciation of the finest textiles such as 'Tulips Hollandaise', designed by A. M. Gourd & Co, which won a gold medal at the 1889 World Fair in Paris. The simple black evening cape with lace detail at the neck was a perfect design to showcase the embroidered tulips.

# JEANNE LANVIN

**PARIS, FRANCE**
1867–1946

**HIGHLIGHTS**
*Robe de style*, floral colours, early sportswear, lavish embroidery.

**DESIGN ETHOS**
Romantic elegance that enhanced feminine attributes without overwhelming the individual personality.

CREDITED AS THE OLDEST PARISIAN FASHION HOUSE STILL IN EXISTENCE AND NAMED AFTER ITS REMARKABLY DETERMINED FOUNDER, MADEMOISELLE JEANNE, THE HOUSE OF LANVIN BUILT ITS SUCCESS ON THE BOND BETWEEN A MOTHER AND HER ONLY DAUGHTER, MARGUERITE MARIE-BLANCHE, WHO BECAME HER INSPIRATIONAL MUSE.

**BELOW:** Portrait of Jeanne Lanvin painted in 1925 by the French artist and illustrator Clementine-Helene Dufau (1869–1973).

Such was the importance of the integral relationship to the prosperity of Lanvin, the company label depicted a graphic illustration by Paul Iribe of a suitably stylish mother figure (Jeanne Lanvin) holding her young child by the hand.

Trained as a seamstress and originally working as a milliner with her own hat shop in Paris, it was the arrival of Marguerite in 1897 that prompted Lanvin to start producing exquisite childrenswear. Based on the ultra-feminine dresses popular in 18th-century portraiture and made from luxurious fabrics in daring colours, Marguerite's refined wardrobe attracted adulation from wealthy admirers who asked to buy similar clothes for their children. The ingenious leap from making beautiful childrenswear to designing comparably stunning womenswear established a new direction for Lanvin, and by 1909, with clothes outselling her bespoke millinery, she created a 'Young Ladies' and Women's Department' where fashionable customers would bring their daughters to choose their outfits together.

Ambitious, hard-working and alive to the ever-changing needs of society, Lanvin incrementally built an empire that included wedding gowns, fur

# JEANNE LANVIN

**ABOVE:** The romantic 'Robe de Style' with its dropped waistline and pretty, full skirt became Lanvin's signature dress, made from moiré silk, with pearl and glass beadwork, embellished with metallic thread embroidery, 1927.

**ABOVE:** Indicative of the dropped waist chemise of the 1920s, this gold evening dress from 1923 details lavish embroidery in a spiral motif, another Lanvin trademark.

collections, menswear, sportswear, perfumes and even home interiors; everything she touched exuded an air of sophisticated elegance.

As the eldest of 11 children born into a working-class family, Lanvin's first steps to self-sufficiency came at the age of 13 with a delivery job for a Parisian milliner who needed her hats dispatched all over the city. Pocketing the bus fare and instead following the omnibus on foot, Lanvin's entrepreneurial spirit was evident from an early age. Working her way up, she secured an apprenticeship with the milliner and by the age of 22 she had saved enough to establish her own boutique on the upper level of a fashion retailer in Rue Boissy d'Anglas. A brief marriage (followed by divorce) to the aristocratic, but financially insecure, Italian Count Emilio di Pietro resulted in the birth of Lanvin's only child, the fortuitous catalyst that defined her professional future.

Maison Lanvin was based in the most fashionable part of Paris with premises at 15 and 22 Rue de Faubourg Saint-Honoré. By this time, Lanvin's extended family had become an essential component of her empire: she employed all ten of her siblings in the house ateliers. At every stage of development – from child, to adolescent, to married woman – Jeanne's daughter remained the iconic inspiration for the designer. Lanvin's most famous aesthetic from the 1920s was a simplified version of the formal court dresses worn in France in the 18th century, known as the *robe de style*. Her modern interpretations utilized a flat-fronted bodice, cap sleeves and a dropped waistline, from which emerged a flattering full skirt. Delicate embroidery and beaded appliqué became a house signature regularly used to embellish Lanvin's pretty dresses. The overall effect was always elegantly decorative without theatrical fussiness.

The artistic sensibilities that fed into Lanvin's work were drawn from many sources. She travelled extensively, taking notes as she went, and global references from Chinese outfits and Spanish *toreador* costumes were incorporated into her designs. She collected antique fabrics to reference textural ideas, was an enthusiastic art collector, with works by Renoir, Degas and Fantin-Latour in her possession, and recreated a bold colour palette that particularly favoured the precise shade of blue endorsed by the Italian fresco painter Fra Angelico.

The company expanded as Lanvin's perpetual curiosity and smart business brain explored new markets. She set up her own dye factory to produce the subtle colours she demanded, designed decorative furnishings and art deco-style *objets* for an interior design shop, was the first couturier to offer made-to-measure menswear, and in 1933, launched Eau de Lanvin – one of the first unisex perfumes to be marketed. Lanvin died peacefully in 1946 at the age of 79. Her daughter Marie-Blanche took over as president of the company.

**ABOVE:** Black satin day dress with matching hat designed in an elaborate bow, 1936.

**OPPOSITE:** Jeanne Lanvin inspects the exquisite decoration stitched by hand on this elegant evening gown, late 1930s.

JEANNE LANVIN

# PAUL POIRET

**PARIS, FRANCE**
1879–1944

**HIGHLIGHTS**
Rejection of the corset, Empire line, jewel-coloured turbans, harem pants, 'Lampshade' tunics.

**DESIGN ETHOS**
Orientalism originated from a theatrical fantasy of the Far East.

FASHION TOOK A MAJOR CHANGE OF DIRECTION AT THE TURN OF THE 20TH CENTURY AND PAUL POIRET, A BRILLIANT SELF-PUBLICIST, BECAME THE LEADING PROPONENT FOR TRANSFORMATIVE IDEAS THAT REFLECTED THE PERIOD.

BELOW: Portrait of the innovative showman Paul Poiret, 1916.

In an era that saw an explosion of haute couture businesses (at least 20 new houses were established between 1900 and 1925), the Parisian fashion designer made his name by rejecting the ladylike neutrals and overblown S-shaped silhouette of the early 1900s, presenting instead a linear vision of striking bold colours and clean cubist lines.

Schiaparelli called him 'the Leonardo of Fashion' thanks to his signature style: over-the-top theatrical exuberance with lavish embroidery, bejewelled headwear and exotic fabrics. His refusal to accept the 'healthy' straight-front corset instigated by Doctor Inès Gâches-Sarraute, and which Poiret called the 'abominable apparatus', was the start of a fashion revolution. In his biography, Poiret wrote: 'It was in the name of Liberty that I proclaimed the fall of the corset.'

Studying classical sculpture at the Musée du Louvre, Poiret recognized a silhouette that supported fabric emanating from the shoulders, flowing in a natural drape around the body. By changing the focus for women's clothing, from the waist to the shoulder line, he would go on to produce comfortable, unrestrictive clothes with a narrower, straighter line that resulted in elegant simplicity. These designs radically impacted the emancipation of women, bringing them greater physical freedom and encouraging them to indulge in sporting activities; he was the first to put women in Persian-inspired jupe-culottes and designed many versions of his 'pantaloon gown'.

# PAUL POIRET

**BELOW:** A variation of Poiret's famous 'Sorbet', creation with hooped tunic worn over a long skirt, using block colour satins and bugle bead embroidery, 1913.

**BELOW:** Exploring ideas of theatrical fashion, Poiret played with unconventional silhouettes, like his shimmering 'zouave' dress with gathered pantaloon hemline.

As the son of a Parisian cloth merchant, Poiret had been born into a world of textiles and from an early age developed skills as an artist and draughtsman. As a teenager, he sold fashion sketches to the house of Madeleine Chéruit, and in 1898 he began training with the couturier Jacques Doucet and, later, Charles Frederick Worth. Opening his own house in 1903,

Poiret's first concepts were simply to make fashion less ostentatious and restrictive, by reducing the number of petticoats under a garment and relaxing the rigidity of the corset. Early designs included a wrapped kimono shape, and dancer and choreographer Isadora Duncan endorsed the loose, flowing garments he favoured.

Curious about the interplay between fashion and

# PAUL POIRET

**OPPOSITE:** Decorative illustrations by Paul Iribe, (1883–1935) commissioned by Poiret for his 1908 fashion book, *Les Robes des Paul Poiret.*

**RIGHT:** 'Irudee' evening dress made from metallic silk and notable for its simplistic construction and low slung tubular rouleau snaking around the hips, 1923.

all other explorations of creativity, Poiret's work was influenced by a major exhibition of the Fauvist artists, who liberally used wild, clashing colours in their paintings, and like many Parisians he embraced the trend for Orientalism. This had been brought to the city by the impresario Sergei Diaghilev and painter and designer Leon Bakst, who designed exotic sets and costumes for their Ballet Russes productions. Poiret too was a flamboyant figure who loved dressing up as the maestro to present his grand view of fashion as an all-encompassing art form. Denise Boulet, his young, slim wife, looked marvellous as his muse, and fashion shows were staged in the formal gardens of the extravagant Faubourg Saint-Honoré Maison he now owned. Poiret's opulent vision was unrivalled in Paris, designing pants for women that were worn for bicycling, harem pantaloons and a '*robe culotte*' similar to a jumpsuit. Conversely, he also somewhat derailed women's emancipation by designing the restrictive 'hobble' skirt. At the famous fancy-dress ball he hosted in 1911, named 'The Thousand and Second Night', his wife showcased a 'lampshade' tunic trimmed with fur that swung concentrically around the body, supported on a wire frame. To publicize his creations, he commissioned artists Paul Iribe, Georges Lepape and Romain de Tirtoff (known under the pseudonym Erté) to create stunning fashion plates to elevate the perception of his endeavours. He also broadened his fashion empire to include decorative interior designs and perfumes.

After World War I, Poiret's wild eccentricities fell out of favour, as fashion took a less opulent turn. He left his own house in 1926 and died on the streets, a penniless vagrant.

# JEAN PATOU

**NORMANDY, FRANCE** 1887–1936

**HIGHLIGHTS**
Jersey sportswear, cubist sweaters, Joy – the 'most expensive perfume in the world'.

**DESIGN ETHOS**
Freedom for women achieved through purity of line.

ONCE DUBBED 'THE MOST ELEGANT MAN IN EUROPE', THE FASHIONABLE FRENCHMAN JEAN PATOU LIVED AN ENVIABLE, HIGH-OCTANE LIFE, SURROUNDED BY FAST CARS, SPEEDBOATS AND GLAMOROUS WOMEN.

BELOW: Portrait of Jean Patou, circa 1910.

Charming, debonair and astute in creating a modern couture house that catered to a celebrity clientele (such as Louise Brooks, Josephine Baker and Mary Pickford), Patou was a pioneer in designing simple, fluid womenswear that flattered the female body and prioritized comfort.

Born in Normandy, France, the only son of a wealthy tanner who made chamois leather for luxury goods, Jean-Alexandre Patou had no interest in following his father's footsteps, and initially tried working as a furrier before setting up his own fashion house in 1914 when he was just 23 years old. This was immediately derailed by the arrival of World War I. Taking inspiration from time spent travelling as a soldier in the Balkans, Patou's early designs, which sold from his salon opened on Armistice Day on Rue Saint-Florentin, consisted of fluid, unrestrictive dresses and sporty separates that did not require a corset. Cubism and the art deco movement were both influential in his desire to create a new modernism in womenswear: he favoured strong, simple lines and vibrant colour and embraced the new technology of machine knitwear, making a collection of cubist-style sweaters, with matching hats, scarves and gloves.

By the middle of the 1920s, Patou's business was flourishing, with a career that rivalled the success of Coco Chanel's. His visit to the USA in 1924 to recruit six slender, flat-chested models, who he felt were better suited to his style of contemporary unrestrictive

# JEAN PATOU

designs than curvy European girls, resulted in a wave of publicity and a boost in sales on both sides of the Atlantic. The inter-war years saw an increase in leisure time that Patou was quick to capitalize on and he opened retail shops selling ready-to-wear beachwear in the seaside resorts of Monte Carlo, Deauville and Cannes. His fashionable wardrobe aimed at women who pursued an active lifestyle also appealed to customers who simply wanted to be stylish spectators. 'The sporty silhouette is absolutely chic,' Patou said of the jersey sportswear, swimwear and daytime pyjamas he designed. A natural self-publicist, he was the first couturier to register his own signature in 1925, and visibly monogram his initials on the outside of his early sportswear garments.

**ABOVE:** Jean Patou selecting American models to bring back to his French atelier. He felt their slimline physiques were better suited to his loose, unrestrictive clothing.

Though utterly elegant and simplistic in line, Patou's clothes were also impeccably made, often with outstanding embroidery, beautiful stitching and attention to detail. Strong colour was a recognizable Patou signature, and owning a dye company allowed him to create shades that were unique to his collections. As a showman and bon viveur, Patou's flamboyant reputation ensured his Parisian shows and the after-parties that followed were glamorous social occasions where he showered guests with free champagne and perfume samples; film stars, sporting heroes and notable aristocrats clamoured to be invited. The stylish wardrobes he designed for the female aviator Ruth Elder and French tennis champion Suzanne Lenglen enhanced his fame and business success internationally.

After the dominance of the Garconne look that dictated fashion trends until the late 1920s, towards the end of the decade it was Patou and not Chanel who reinstated the natural waistline and lengthened hemlines to the ankles for a collection of beautifully cut evening dresses, restoring a feminine elegance to fashion. With legs demurely covered, Patou focused on a new erogenous zone, with many of his stunning evening gowns designed to expose shoulders and reveal a bare back with a dramatic deep-cut V.

Patou's famous fragrance, Joy, marketed as 'the costliest perfume in the world', was debuted in 1930 to help relaunch the brand after the devastating financial impact of the Great Depression. His untimely death in 1936 at the age of 48 undoubtedly contributed to the designer's personal lack of recognition within a broader sense. The house, now owned by Louis Vuitton Moet Hennessy (LVMH) and renamed as Patou, is under the control of Guillaume Henry.

# JEAN PATOU

**OPPOSITE LEFT:** Sporty beachwear made from jersey fabric became a Patou staple in the 1920s.

**OPPOSITE RIGHT:** A dropped-waist, button-through day dress, illustrated for a 1923 advertisement.

**RIGHT:** Endorsement by French film actress Arlette Marchal boosted Patou's reputation. She is seen wearing a self-striped devoré evening gown in this 1935 portrait taken by Austrian fashion photographer Madame d'Ora (Dora Kallmus 1881–1963).

# CHARLES JAMES

**SANDHURST, ENGLAND**
1906–1978

**HIGHLIGHTS**
'Four Leaf Clover' ball gown, asymmetric cutting, voluminous satin 'eiderdown' jacket.

**DESIGN ETHOS**
Sculptural construction for the body to create an ultra-feminine silhouette.

FETED AS A FASHION GENIUS, AND CONSISTENTLY REFERRED TO WITHIN THE INDUSTRY AS 'THE COUTURIER'S COUTURIER' (BALENCIAGA CALLED HIM 'THE WORLD'S BEST'), THE COMPLICATED PERSONALITY OF ANGLO-AMERICAN CHARLES JAMES DETRACTED FROM HIS UNIQUE ARTISTRY, WHICH UNDOUBTEDLY CONTRIBUTED TO A WIDER LACK OF RECOGNITION BY THE WORLD.

**BELOW:** A masterful mix of contrasting textures, silk chiffon, silk faille and Dupont nylon tulle are used to create a dramatic silhouette for this 1954 'Butterfly' ballgown.

With an architectural approach to design, James was a pioneer in terms of garment construction and innovative shaping. His long-standing career hit its zenith in the late 1940s and early 1950s, an era that celebrated an idealized version of feminine beauty. James excelled in Glamour with a capital G. His extraordinary complex ball gowns underpinned by a lightweight infrastructure created a dynamic silhouette for a range of high society beauties on both sides of the Atlantic. Expert cutting, an experimental use of colour and a unique method of draping fabric around the female form were techniques utilized to produce his elegant, often asymmetrical, evening wear.

Charles James had a privileged, but difficult, upbringing in England, born to an aristocratic family, with an American heiress mother and a disciplinarian English father. At the age of 18 he was packed off to family friends in Chicago, where he worked briefly in the architectural design department of a utilities company. By his early twenties, with no formal training, he was designing and selling hats through his own millinery shop, under the name 'Charles

# CHARLES JAMES

**RIGHT:** Charles James in his atelier, fitting a dark crimson silk taffeta evening gown for his client Austine Hearst, the wife of the millionaire publishing magnate, Randolph Hearst Jnr. Late 1940s.

Boucheron'. His love affair with hats continued throughout his life and the principles he perfected for millinery, of moulding and manipulating fabric around a rigid form, were later adopted for his couture collections.

An innovator in many fields, his creations were conceived as sculptural artworks with James fascinated by the fluidity of different fabrics and new advancements in technology. His wraparound dress known as the 'Taxi' dress was designed with very few seams and a couple of strategic hooks to hold it together; so quick and easy to throw on, it could be done in the back of a cab. He created structure through layering fabrics, experimented with bias draping and made intricate seaming appear invisible. Inventively, he used the zipper fastening (previously used only for underwear and luggage) as a decorative feature, wrapping it around the torso in a novel way. Couture garments were his forte, but he also produced clothes sold through the accessories department of Best &

**LEFT:** The 'Tree' dress from 1957, enhanced the female form through meticulous corsetry. Pale pink taffeta is offset with a flourish of vibrant colour at the hem.

**BELOW:** The evening dress named as 'Clover' by James, with four distinct shaped panels making up the skirt, shown alongside its under garment with complex stitching and stiff interfacings.

**OPPOSITE:** Thought to be James's favourite design, this full-length version of the Clover Dress became a classic. It is made from white Duchesse satin and black *velours de Lyon*, with extravagant skirt panels which, from above, fan out to look like a four-leaf clover.

Co. in Manhattan, later establishing contracts to sell ready-to-wear pieces through some of the biggest stores in America, including Lord & Taylor and Bergdorf Goodman.

In 1930, James opened his own couture house in London's Bruton Street, but financial instability was a constant presence and in subsequent years he frequently transferred business operations between London, New York and Paris, never settling long enough to establish continuity. Despite setbacks, his originality continued to attract A-list Hollywood stars such as Marlene Dietrich and was applauded by other couturiers; Elsa Schiaparelli was a fan.

James disliked prints but was a gifted colourist, successfully mixing unusual combinations, and often using different weights of fabric – velvets, satins

## CHARLES JAMES

and taffeta – in the same colour hues to create light and shade within a dress. He was best known for a remarkable white satin evening jacket from 1937 that resembled a sculptural eiderdown with exaggerated padded shoulder details, and his sumptuous 'Four Leaf Clover' gown from 1953, which was made up of 30 pattern pieces and yards of fabric yet still retained a lightness of touch.

Persistent talk of lawsuits and bankruptcy overshadowed all James' business ventures, and for all the glowing endorsements received from high society and fashion magazines such as *Vogue* and *Harper's Bazaar*, the rumours of a volatile, self-sabotaging personality rumbled on.

By the 1970s, James was broke, living in a bedsit in the Chelsea Hotel in New York. In awe of his talent, Halston created a position for him as an assistant, but James was a problematic employee, and the collaborative role was short-lived. His legacy remains that of 'tortured fashion genius'.

# GABRIELLE CHANEL

**SAUMUR, FRANCE** 1883–1971

**HIGHLIGHTS**
Little black dress, jersey suits, decorative costume jewellery, two-tone shoes.

**DESIGN ETHOS**
Understated elegance that allowed freedom of movement.

THE COMPLICATED TWISTS AND TURNS OF GABRIELLE (COCO) CHANEL'S NARRATIVE ARE FAR MORE DRAMATIC THAN ANY OF THE HOLLYWOOD FILMS THAT HAVE BEEN MADE ABOUT HER LIFE, AND MORE THAN HALF A DECADE SINCE HER DEATH SHE REMAINS THE MOST FAMOUS NAME IN FASHION HISTORY.

BELOW: Gabrielle 'Coco' Chanel in the South of France wearing one of the Breton jerseys she helped to popularize.

The signature tropes she wore herself have become a byword for elegance and style: the Little Black Dress (LBD), a perfectly proportioned boxy suit, the 2.55 quilted handbag, luminous pearls and two-tone shoes.

All Chanel inventions, originated in part as a result of the frustration she directed towards the male couturiers of the day, have stood the test of time. She rejected the idea that women should be subjugated to the restrictive corsets and cartwheel hats of the belle époque era, and loathed the bright theatrical clothes that Paul Poiret promoted. 'Let us beware of originality in couture,' she said. 'It leads to costume.' Her instinctive response was to offer a more relaxed aesthetic for women: comfortable, easy clothes such as jersey cardigans and long skirts in a muted colour palette provided practical solutions in a changing female world.

Chanel endured a miserable childhood, abandoned with her two sisters, at the age of 12, into an orphanage convent in south-west France, following the premature death of her mother. At the age of 20 she moved into the large chateau of a wealthy playboy; determined to make her own money, she started to sell straw boater hats, bought from Galeries Lafayette and decorated with a simple bow ribbon, to the glamorous women

# GABRIELLE CHANEL

**ABOVE:** Early examples of Chanel's relaxed jersey suits, published in *Les Elegances Parisiennes* in March 1917.

**ABOVE:** The first range of Little Black Dresses appeared in 1926, endorsing Chanel's philosophy of understated elegance. Pearl earrings, and the single strand pearl necklace shown here, became a signature for the house.

who visited the chateau. Buoyed by the success of her modest hats, in 1910 she opened her first shop, Chanel Modes, the first of many retail premises in Rue Cambon, with number 31 still the flagship Chanel store. Despite the disruption of World War I, expansion came rapidly and within a few years she had opened retail premises selling unstructured, comfortable casualwear in Deauville, Biarritz and Cannes.

Wartime restrictions required innovative thinking. Chanel bought cheap cotton jersey (intended for men's underwear) from manufacturer Jean Rodier and turned it into high fashion. Her elegant sportswear, casual fisherman's blouses, hip-length cardigan jackets and straight tunics were a revelation. 'Everything she does makes news' said *Vogue*, who in 1917 called her 'The House of Jersey'.

Post-war living required a new simplicity, and Chanel was at the forefront of a revolution, becoming a trailblazer for her own designs. She cut her hair into a short bob, designed vest-like knitted bathing suits that revealed enough flesh to cultivate a suntan, and cleverly decorated plain black fabrics with intricate machine embroidery provided by a workforce from the expatriate Russian community who had escaped to Paris, to produce her 'Slavic' collection. Her Jazz

Age tubular flapper dresses, cut daringly short to accommodate the craze for dancing and constructed from one piece of fabric to skim the body and avoid ugly seams, were the height of fashion in the early 1920s. In 1926, she presented a new black crepe de Chine dress. The original LBD was to become a wardrobe staple for women everywhere but at the time it was derided for its austerity by Paul Poiret as '*poverty de luxe*', to which Chanel replied, 'Never confuse poverty with simplicity.'

She also instigated the trend for conspicuous costume jewellery, although she only wore the real thing herself, gifts bestowed upon her by numerous wealthy men. Nothing derailed her success until World War II in 1939, when Chanel chose to close her business. In 1945, she retreated to Switzerland for ten years, independently wealthy from the money she received from her best-selling perfume, Chanel N°5. Her fury at the success of Monsieur Dior's 1947 'New Look' propelled her comeback and in 1954, at the age of 71 she reopened her atelier. The collection

**ABOVE LEFT:** An early advertisement for Chanel No 5, illustrated by the great Georges Goursat, known professionally as Sem (1863–1934)

**ABOVE RIGHT:** Experimenting with colour in 1938, this evening ensemble made from fluid wool jersey featured in an autumn issue of *Marie Claire* magazine.

**RIGHT:** A kaleidoscope of Chanel suits on show at the V&A museum in London, as part of their successful exhibition *Gabrielle Chanel. Fashion Manifesto,* in September 2023.

# GABRIELLE CHANEL

of softly tailored tweed suits, with collarless boxy jackets and skirts that grazed below the knee, were championed initially by an American market, but later became a stylish uniform for all women. Chanel never retired. At the age of 88, she was working on a new collection the day before she died.

Complex, sometimes controversial, ambitious and charismatic, Chanel successfully elevated her status in society from tradesperson to 'celebrity', collaborating with the great artists of the day, socializing with royalty and prime ministers, while visually consolidating her reputation as the stylish modern figurehead of her own label. She remains one of the most famous fashion designers of all time.

# MADAME GRÈS

**PARIS, FRANCE**
1903–1993

**HIGHLIGHTS**
'Goddess' silk jersey dresses, sumptuous use of fabric to create perfect draping.

**DESIGN ETHOS**
Sculptural fluidity inspired by the purity of classical Greek antiquity.

FOREVER ASSOCIATED WITH THE CLASSICAL ELEGANCE OF THE 1930S, MADAME GRÈS (WHO ALSO WORKED UNDER THE NAME MAISON ALIX) IS BEST KNOWN FOR HER BEAUTIFUL DRAPED JERSEY DRESSES THAT INTRICATELY SWATHED COLUMNS OF FABRIC AROUND THE BODY.

**BELOW:** Madame Grès, photographed in Great Britain in 1968.

Her couture skills used to create a purity of line, achieved through masterful manipulation of fabric into perfect pleats, resulted in neoclassical silhouettes that resembled Greek sculpture. As such, she was adored by the stars of Hollywood's silver screen – Greta Garbo, Jean Harlow and Marlene Dietrich – for her ability to turn them into real-life goddesses.

Many of her gowns appeared deceptively simple, such was the fluidity of the finish she achieved, but in reality, it was the meticulous gathering, pleating and expert cutting techniques she perfected that defined her distinctive style. With total disregard for what other Parisian designers were doing, dismissive of fashion 'trends' and oblivious to outside influences, Grès continually evolved her vision from season to season, convinced that her fusion of sensuality and classicism had a timeless longevity. Working solely in the traditions of haute couture, her techniques required hours of fitting time for each client. 'A couture dress is a second skin. I like to accentuate the beauty, the personality and the individual gestures of the women I dress,' she said.

Predominantly using fabrics that had a soft handle, such as crepe de Chine and silk jersey, Grès' flowing designs often incorporated surprising glimpses of flesh, revealed behind the loosely gathered folds;

# MADAME GRÈS

**LEFT:** Simple fluid lines typify the work of Madame Grès, as seen in the clever construct of this deep pink and green jersey evening dress, with contrasting grey hood cut seamlessly into the finished piece.

bare shoulders, a backless cut-out and a thigh-high split became her house signatures. Though she often favoured a monochrome colour palette that included black, white, nude and ivory, Grès was not afraid to work with strong colour, surprising her clientele with vibrant orange, lilac and rose pink.

Madame Grès, who was born Germaine Émilie Krebs, had an artistic education studying painting and sculpture in Paris, with ambitions to be a classical sculptor. Her family discouraged this idea and instead at the age of 21 she began a career in fashion, with a three-month apprenticeship designing toiles (mock-ups) for the French house of Premet. Having changed her name to Alix, she opened her first couture house in 1933 in partnership with Julie Barton. The company, Alix-Barton, disbanded after a year, by which time it had already established a reputation for simplistic styles based on flowing lines.

Grès continued to produce high-end clothing under the name Alix, and her unique talent for

# MADAME GRÈS

**OPPOSITE:** The intricate cutting and fabric manipulation of Madame Grès are exemplified in the pleated crossover bodice, from the Spring/Summer collection, 1963.

**BELOW RIGHT:** Silk jersey expertly cut into a multi-colored 'woven' bodice and perfectly draped column skirt and cape, 1959.

draping was often featured in fashion editorials; the German photographer Horst P. Horst took dramatic black-and-white images for *Vogue* magazine in 1938 of 'Alix's Grecian white jersey' evening gown. She refused to design clothes for the wives of German officers during World War II, and consequently had her business shut down, whereupon she took herself off to the Pyrenees, bought cloth from the market and continued to drape fabric into clothes using a dummy made from a bale of hay and a piece of wood.

Following the war, the reinvention of her business resumed. Having reworked her Russian husband's name Serge Czerefkov into a new moniker, she emerged as Madame Grès. Working only on live mannequins, Grès' preferred methods of construction involved physically placing as much as 60 metres (65 yards) of fabric into position on the body. She would often only use two lengths of fabric to create an evening gown, cutting with precision, rarely sewing things together, and taking many hours of subtle manipulation to achieve the perfect pleats she required. Her Grecian-inspired 'Goddess' dresses that clung sensuously to the body were underpinned with almost invisible boned bodices to ensure structural support.

Unprepared to compromise her exacting standards, she had no time for couturiers who diversified into ready-to-wear collections, although during the 1950s her aesthetic became more tailored, and she produced soft suits for women, often with asymmetric details and loose dolman sleeves. Her lifelong passion for travel influenced her designs: the geometric cut of the kimono and kaftan shapes were visible in clothes she produced in the 1960s and 1970s when she began experimenting with square cuts. With a career that spanned more than five decades, her influence persists long after her death.

# ELSA SCHIAPARELLI

**ROME, ITALY**
1890–1973

**HIGHLIGHTS**
Collaborations with the surrealist artists, invention of Shocking Pink, 'Skeleton Dress', 'Shoe Hat'.

**DESIGN ETHOS**
Theatrical collections thematically designed, with prints, jewellery, buttons and accessories styled to complement the imaginative storyline.

IN PARIS IN THE 1930S, A DIMINUTIVE ITALIAN AFFECTIONATELY KNOWN AS 'SCHIAP' ARRIVED ON THE SCENE TO CHALLENGE THE UNDISPUTED DOMINANCE OF GABRIELLE CHANEL.

**ABOVE:** Elsa Schiaparelli in her early 40s, taken by the society photographer Alexander 'Sasha' Stewart.

**OPPOSITE:** Influenced by the surrealist artists who were her friends, Schiaparelli created a series of hats shaped like other objects. This black and pink felt wool 'Shoe Hat' was perhaps her most talked about design.

The two women moved within the same artistic circles, but the opposing styles they endorsed resulted in a vociferous rivalry, with Chanel dismissing Elsa Schiaparelli as 'that Italian artist who makes clothes'. Schiaparelli offered an alternative to the loose, unstructured shift dresses of the 1920s by providing a return to elegant tailoring, emphasizing a narrow silhouette and structured shoulder line. Her use of extravagant colour and outstanding decorative embellishments upended the minimalism of '*le style garçon*' and provided women with sophisticated glamour.

Schiaparelli also set a precedent that was copied by future generations of designers when she embarked on a series of collaborations that aligned the worlds of fashion and art.

Her fertile imagination responded to the unsettling motifs of the surrealist artists; intrigued by their visual shock tactics, she found skilful ways to incorporate subversive ideas into her own work, notably in her silk crêpe 'Skeleton' evening dress that featured prominent ribcage 'bones' on the front and back of the bodice. The bizarre dress, which referenced some of Salvador Dalí's work, caused an outrage (as she intended), as did her unusual collection of millinery. This included the 'Bird Cage Hat', which enclosed a small canary, and the 'Shoe Hat' (Dalí's wife Gala had been photographed with a shoe on her head). Humour and vivid colour infiltrated many of Schiaparelli's designs and she will forever be associated with Shocking Pink, a brilliant

ELSA SCHIAPARELLI

**LEFT:** With its shockingly suggestive lobster print designed by Salvador Dali and made into fabric by the revered silk manufacturer Sache, this dress became famous when Wallis Simpson wore it in a 1937 *Vogue* feature.

**OPPOSITE LEFT:** A collaboration with Schiaparelli's friend Jean Cocteau in 1937 resulted in the *trompe l'oeil* line drawing of two female profiles and a vase of silk roses embellished onto the back of a purple silk evening coat, perfectly executed by Maison Lesage, the oldest embroidery atelier in Paris.

**OPPOSITE RIGHT:** The Zodiac collection from 1938 included this shocking pink 'Phoebus' cape, made from Italian wool and decorated with gold thread and sequins.

shade she invented after much experimentation, to create something that would startle her customers and make the world pay attention to her designs.

Born in Rome to a privileged, ultra-conservative family, Schiaparelli's childhood was full of crazy antics and self-inflicted melodrama; once she threw herself out of a window clutching an umbrella that she thought would act as a parachute. Headstrong and wildly eccentric, at the age of 29 she found herself in New York with a baby daughter to take care of, and an absent husband. Returning to Paris, ostensibly to find specialist medical treatment for her daughter,

# ELSA SCHIAPARELLI

Schiaparelli surrounded herself with the Dada collective of artists, poets and photographers and pondered how to harness her own creative energy into fashion or theatrical costumes as a way to earn a living. Modest success came from a simple black-and-white knitted sweater, with an impressive *trompe l'oeil* bow she designed for herself, but that gave little indication of the dazzling flamboyance that was to come.

With no formal training, early sporty pieces, which she sold from her first shop 'Schiaparelli Pour le Sport' in 1928, were designed with strong architectural shapes and bold patterns influenced by cubism. Her friendships with Jean Cocteau, Christian Bérard and Salvador Dalí resulted is some of her most sensational creations, with the artist's fluid line drawings perfectly transposed by La Maison Lesage into delicate embroideries using gold thread, sequins, gemstones and pearls for Schiaparelli's evening wear. The controversial lobster print designed for the infamous evening gown worn by Wallis Simpson in 1937 was conceived by Dalí, and Schiaparelli's 'Desk Suit' collection, designed with multiple pockets, and her ripped 'Tears' dress that suggested the fabric itself had been repeatedly torn into strips both came directly from Dalí artworks. Indeed, surrealism infiltrated many of her original designs; sunglasses with outsized fluffy eyelashes, plexiglass chokers adorned with colourful metal insects and evening gloves with long red snakeskin fingernails were just some of her improbable ideas.

She was also the first couturier to popularize themed collections, on topics such as music, the zodiac, pagan themes and commedia dell'arte, with every facet of the design process explored for maximum theatrical effect. The 1938 'Circus' collection included buttons shaped as acrobats and flying horses, pirouetting elephants reproduced in embroidery, and a riotous clash of multicoloured silk prints depicting white rabbits and carousel creatures.

Schiaparelli closed her business during World War II and attempts to relaunch in 1945 never quite took off. She showed her final collection in 1954 and released her autobiography *Shocking Life* in the same year.

# CRISTÓBAL BALENCIAGA

**GETARIA, SPAIN**
1895–1972

**HIGHLIGHTS**
The 'Barrel' line, the 'Balloon' skirt, the 'Sack' dress.

**DESIGN ETHOS**
Rejection of excess in favour of elegance, simplicity and fluidity.

IN AN ERA WHEN SUCCESSFUL COUTURIERS WERE HONOURED AS FASHION DICTATORS WHO AUTHORITATIVELY DECREED THE TRENDS OF HIGH SOCIETY, SPANISH DESIGNER CRISTÓBAL BALENCIAGA WAS CONSIDERED AN ABSOLUTE GOD OF HAUTE COUTURE.

**BELOW:** The stylish Spaniard Cristóbal Balenciaga.

The aristocratic photographer Cecil Beaton wrote in 1958, 'Balenciaga, who of all dressmakers is today, the most revered and influential', while French designer Emanuel Ungaro credited him as the Spaniard 'who laid the foundations of modernity' and Hubert de Givenchy, who worked in the atelier alongside him in the 1950s, said simply, 'He is our master.'

The countless accolades received during his longstanding career confirmed his brilliance, but his reputation as a genius who created perfect lines of sculptural minimalism has not diminished during the intervening years. Recognized as the master of elimination, Balenciaga rejected fussy detailing in favour of elegant fluidity, achieved through his unique methods of pattern cutting and choice of fabric. Austere lines, voluminous shapes, bold colours and inspired methods of construction were the aesthetic signatures that identified his work. His body-skimming shapes, which did much to release women from the tyranny of restrictive clothing, were revolutionary at the time, as well as being highly influential in predicting the future direction of modern fashion.

Balenciaga ignited his flair for fashion at an early stage, watching his seamstress mother at work creating outfits for her high society clients; by the age of 14 he was employed as an apprentice to a tailor in San Sebastián, Spain, and he was soon able to precisely

# CRISTÓBAL BALENCIAGA

**RIGHT:** Endlessly influenced by his Spanish heritage, frilled flamenco style dresses were evident in some of Balenciaga's *oeuvre*, as in this dramatic black and white cotton evening dress, from 1951.

copy and make up couture clothes. By the age of 24 he had established a dressmaking and tailoring house under his own name, steadily building a reputation for excellent workmanship and imaginative shapes. He eventually expanded his business to three couture houses, whose clientele included members of the Spanish royal family. Civil war forced him to leave his homeland and move to Paris, where in 1937 he set up new couture premises on Avenue George V and presented his first Parisian collection. Taking inspiration from his own heritage, collections included embroidered boleros, reimagined from the splendid costumes of the bull-fighting *toreador*s, ruffled skirts reminiscent of flamenco dresses, and his famous 1939 'Infanta' gown inspired by the brilliance of Diego Velazquez's *Las Meninas* portrait (1656). The innovative 'Infanta' dress, cut from heavyweight satin, was less exaggerated than the wide-hipped farthingale

**LEFT:** Photographed while rehearsing for a TV show, *Fashions from Paris*, much of Balenciaga's work in the 1950s focused on volume and silhouette.

**OPPOSITE LEFT:** A rose cotton velvet strapless evening dress worn with a jewelled black lace jacket, 1955.

**OPPOSITE RIGHT:** A balloon shaped evening dress fashioned from forest green silk gazaar, with voluminous matching cape, 1961.

# CRISTÓBAL BALENCIAGA

original depicted in the painting but still served as a positive acknowledgement of the artistic influences of Spanish culture.

A decade later, despite the triumph of Dior's feminine 'New Look' in 1947, it was Balenciaga who continued to astound the press and public with his strong sense of colour (lots of black, browns, shades of white, reds, pinks and turquoise blue), his masterful cuts and complex constructions that involved only minimal seams and favoured freedom of movement. Balenciaga did not sketch out his designs, but instead expertly manipulated sumptuous fabrics on to a body, creating a series of evolving shapes that framed women with wearable architecture rather than hugging the female form. Rejecting the popular hourglass silhouette, the 'Barrel' or 'Cocoon' shape emerged first, with a soft cut for three-quarter-length jackets and coats that skimmed the waistline. Later, his popular chemise dress (the 'Sack') eliminated it altogether.

Smocks and tunics made in linen for summer and tweed for winter provided unrestrictive ease for the wearer, and his gravity-defying black 'Balloon' dress with a matching cape made from taffeta offered a dramatic silhouette that challenged traditional tailoring. Simplification of line came with narrower capes and sack dresses, as well as his 1957 triangular 'Baby Doll' lace dresses, which foreshadowed the swinging shift dresses of the 1960s.

A private man who shunned the limelight, Balenciaga would spend hours in his atelier working on a garment to ensure perfection. He rejected the idea of American mass-market technology, preferring to maintain independence to assure standards of luxury and elegance. In 1968, when France experienced student riots and social uprising, Balenciaga decided to close his couture house, aware that the youthquake generation of women demanded an altogether different approach to fashion.

# CHRISTIAN DIOR

**NORMANDY, FRANCE** 1905–1957

**HIGHLIGHTS**
The 'New Look', flowery 'Tulip' silhouette, luxury beading.

**DESIGN ETHOS**
Perfectly proportioned feminine elegance.

NEVER IN THE HISTORY OF HAUTE COUTURE HAS THE JUDGEMENTAL FASHION PENDULUM SWUNG QUITE SO DRAMATICALLY AS IT DID IN 1947.

Against the backdrop of post-war austerity, where womenswear remained influenced by forces' uniforms, Christian Dior, a self-effacing designer from the French provinces, staged a one-man revolution in his debut show with his 'La Ligne Corolle'. Rejecting the suppressive utilitarian shapes created by Schiaparelli's boxy shoulders, narrow skirts and clumpy shoes in favour of something altogether different, his first collection celebrated an idealized version of femininity that aimed to make women look as pretty as flowers. The audience present in the salon of his newly established couture house were ecstatic at what they saw as ladylike elegance, after so many years of drab restrictions.

Dior's graceful silhouette incorporated gently sloping shoulders and a rounded bosom, fashioned in the form of a neatly buttoned peplum 'Bar' jacket that visually accentuated a tiny waist before the shape blossomed out into a full skirt that fell below the knee. It was Carmel Snow, the revered editor-in-chief at *Harper's Bazaar*, who immediately coined the phrase 'New Look'.

The impact of Dior's new line transformed fashion, with every other designer quickly following his lead to produce strikingly similar silhouettes that dominated

**RIGHT:** Dior's New Look in 1947 changed the shape of fashion. The peplum 'Bar' jacket emphasized a tiny waistline, worn over a full skirt that flared gently over the hips, creating an ultra-feminine silhouette.

**OPPOSITE:** Monsieur Christian Dior, the most famous couturier in the world, with a model wearing 'Blenheim', from a range of satin evening gowns.

# CHRISTIAN DIOR

the female wardrobe for the best part of a decade. With successive collections, Dior consolidated his reputation, and by the 1950s he was internationally acknowledged as the most famously influential and financially successful couturier.

Christian Dior came from a wealthy background and spent his very early years growing up in a seaside town on the coast of Normandy before moving to Paris at the age of five. Ambitions to be an architect were vetoed by his parents and instead he went to the École de Science Politiques in Paris to study political science. At the age of 25 he was drafted into the French army for a short while, before working as an art dealer, and then as an illustrator for fashion magazines and newspapers. His first couture experience came with Robert Piguet, where he worked as an in-house designer alongside Pierre Balmain. During the war years he found employment with Lucien Lelong, one of the few French couture houses to stay open during this time, and it was at this much larger couture house that Dior perfected his cutting skills.

In 1946, the millionaire textile magnate Marcel Boussac – thought to be the wealthiest man in France at the time – approached Dior with a suggestion that he should relaunch Philippe et Gaston, a successful couture house from the 1920s. Dior refused the offer but negotiated backing for a house in his own name, located on the prestigious Avenue Montaigne. Success was immediate, and new themes were invented for every subsequent collection: the 'Oblique' line, the 'Tulip' line, the 'H' line, the 'A' line, the 'Arrow' line – ideas that women in the fashion-conscious 1950s were happy to try out even if the clothes were uncomfortably demanding to wear. The Dior aesthetic remained unapologetically feminine with a slim waist (usually accentuated with a wide waistband) and a hemline that fell below the knee, but his expertise lay in changing proportions and creating shape. Volume came from stiffened petticoats and pleated skirts, boned corsets provided a perfect uplift for breasts and pulled the waist tighter, and collars shot up off the body in gravity-defying angles. Surprisingly, he made use of men's pinstripe suiting and houndstooth check in some of his more streamlined suits.

However, global fame and pressure to constantly produce new ideas contributed to Dior's health problems, and he died suddenly and unexpectedly at the age of 52 at an Italian spa clinic he was attending to lose weight. Yves Saint Laurent was appointed as his immediate successor, and in the intervening years there have been many others at the helm of what is considered the most famous couture house in Paris, including John Galliano, Raf Simons and Maria Grazia Chiuri.

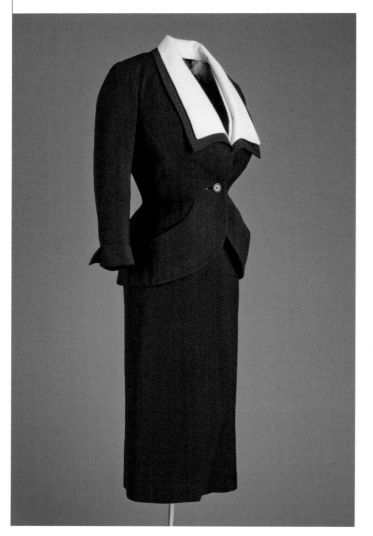

**LEFT:** Navy wool crepe suit with contrast white collar, 1951.

**OPPOSITE:** Dior's successful aesthetic exemplified in swathes of Duchesse satin, with fur trim details, as photographed for *Picture Post* 1954.

# CHRISTIAN DIOR

# HUBERT DE GIVENCHY

**BEAUVAIS, FRANCE** 1927–2018

**HIGHLIGHTS**
Bettina blouse, 'Little Black Dress', the 'Sack' dress.

**DESIGN ETHOS**
Purity of line that prioritized simplicity over embellishment.

ONE OF THE GREAT FRENCH ARISTOCRATIC COUTURIERS WHO DOMINATED THE 1950S FASHION SCENE AT A TIME WHEN PARIS STILL DICTATED TRENDS TO THE REST OF THE WORLD, HUBERT DE GIVENCHY WAS AS ELEGANT AND REFINED AS THE CLOTHES HE DESIGNED IN HIS PARISIAN ATELIER.

**BELOW:** Hubert James Taffin de Givenchy with his favourite Afghan hound.

In a decade that was transitional, with new shapes and silhouettes redefined season after season, Givenchy presented structured simplicity, designing clothes that were guaranteed to flatter the young women he favoured, crafted from sublime cutting techniques and supple fabrics.

Born in Beauvais, France, to an aristocratic family, Givenchy briefly attempted to study law before changing career paths, and by the age of 20 he was taking drawing lessons at the École des Beaux-Arts in Paris. He worked for several couturiers, including Jacques Fath, Robert Piguet and Lucien Lelong, and from 1947 he spent four years working for Elsa Schiaparelli before setting up a small house of his own in 1952. The future he predicted lay in relaxed separates that were comfortable to wear but still looked chic. Men's cotton shirting fabric became a staple, used for the ruffle-sleeved 'Bettina' blouse (named after the famous model Bettina Graziani) in his first collection of skirts and blouses, which was critically acclaimed for its youthful impact.

Givenchy championed softer lines, in contrast to the rigidity of Dior's enforced femininity, and towards the end of the 1950s he was pushing the fluctuating waistline aside to the point of logical conclusion, and presented the 'Sack' dress that relied on the female body to provide shape. In the fashion-conscious

# HUBERT DE GIVENCHY

1950s, his 1957 waistless 'chemise' was dressed up with the addition of a hat, jewellery and gloves to conform to the decade's desire for aesthetic formality. This unrestrictive line proved revolutionary for young women, as the next generation of designers pushed the idea of modern tunic styles that simply skimmed the body.

**ABOVE:** Named after the most popular model of the day, Bettina Graziani, Givenchy's 'Bettina' blouse originally made from men's shirting, became a house success story for decades.

**LEFT:** A 1950s black suit cut to mid-calf, with detailed rose embroidery.

**OPPOSITE LEFT:** Audrey Hepburn, Givenchy's most famous muse, in a still from the 1954 film *Sabrina*.

**OPPOSITE RIGHT:** One of the most iconic images of Audrey Hepburn in a little black dress designed specifically for the movie *Breakfast at Tiffany's*. Their friendship endured a lifetime, and Hepburn championed all Givenchy's clothes, on and off screen.

His admiration for the architectural simplicity of Spanish master Cristóbal Balenciaga greatly influenced Givenchy's own design ethos, and when Givenchy established a larger couture house opposite his revered idol on Avenue George V, the two men became great friends. At Balenciaga's suggestion they would preview each other's collections to provide professional critique, and long after Balenciaga's death, Givenchy would view each new collection and ask himself, 'What would Cristóbal think of this? Is it more than it needs to be?'

Ahead of his time, Givenchy was inspired by modern art and strived to provide a purity that eliminated excessive decoration. In 1958, he was quoted as calling himself 'a classicist working in the modern genre'. He was one of the first couturiers to create a total look for his clients, opening the Givenchy Nouvelle Boutique in 1968 selling high-end ready-to-wear clothes that reinforced his no-fuss philosophy; denim dresses, double-breasted raincoats, culotte pants and comfy sweaters were all successfully targeted at a younger demographic.

Aside from his clothes, Givenchy was best known for his 40-year relationship, both on and off the screen, with gamine movie star Audrey Hepburn, who proved to be his perfect muse. The contemporary understated outfits she wore in the 1954 movie *Sabrina* helped elevate both their reputations. With Hepburn loyally choosing Givenchy offstage, she became a model brand ambassador, applauded for her style on many 'Best Dressed' lists. Credited with designing the iconic 'Little Black Dress' for Hepburn's role of Holly Golightly in the 1961 film *Breakfast at Tiffany's*, Givenchy's reputation soared higher, opening up lucrative doors to a wealthy American market, where he catered for a slew of Hollywood movie stars, including Lauren Bacall, Elizabeth Taylor and Greta Garbo, as well as Jacqueline Kennedy.

Throughout the 1960s, his global fame spread, and he branched out commercially into menswear, as well as retailing perfumes, handbags, shoes and accessories. By the mid-1970s he had become the most influential designer of the 20th century, diversifying into furnishing fabrics, homeware, hotel interiors and even luxury cars, designing for the Ford Motor Company and Nissan. In 1988, Givenchy sold his company to LVMH. He retired in 1996.

# HUBERT DE GIVENCHY

# CLAIRE McCARDELL

**MARYLAND, USA** 1905–58

**HIGHLIGHTS**
The 'Pop Over' dress, sports playsuit, leotards, coloured topstitching.

**DESIGN ETHOS**
Pioneer of American leisurewear; pared-down practicality using functional fabrics.

AT THE BEGINNING OF THE 20TH CENTURY, PARIS REMAINED THE UNDISPUTED FASHION CAPITAL OF THE WORLD, BUT ADVANCES IN TECHNOLOGY LEADING TO MASS-MARKET PRODUCTION PROVIDED DESIGNERS IN THE USA WITH AN OPPORTUNITY TO CAPITALIZE ON NEW IDEAS OF MODERN CASUALWEAR.

**BELOW:** Claire McCardell in one of her own designs.

More than anyone else, Claire McCardell, who designed with herself in mind, was instrumental in inventing the type of laid-back, comfortable sportwear we now associate with many of America's leading designers. Her self-belief resulted in functional clothes that were not only elegant in their simplicity, but could also be versatile. Many items had adjustable components, such as a drawstring waist that could be configured to suit different body shapes, and the individual wearer was encouraged to mix and match her interchangeable trousers, skirts and blouses in the style of a capsule collection. 'I've always designed things I needed for myself. It just turns out that other people need them too,' she told Babs Simpson from *Vogue*.

McCardell was interested in fashion from an early age but, discouraged by her father, she studied home economics instead at Hood College, a girls' school in Frederick, Maryland. At the age of 21, she started at Parsons School of Design in New York, which included a period of study at the Paris campus. On graduation, she worked first as a sketcher in a dress shop and then as an assistant to Richard Turk, a freelance designer. When he secured employment at the mid-market clothing manufacturer Townley Frocks, McCardell went with him. Turk subsequently died suddenly in

# CLARE McCARDELL

tragic circumstances and McCardell was appointed as chief designer, a position that allowed her to launch a quiet revolution in easy, inexpensive clothes.

Her first big success was the 'Monastic' – a seemingly free-flowing tent dress cut on the bias, with no shoulder pads, bust darts or shaping at the waist. It had little hanger appeal but with the addition of a tie belt and a body, transformed into something every woman in America wanted to wear. The 'Monastic' was so phenomenally successful that the company went bust, overwhelmed with production problems needed

**ABOVE LEFT:** Stylish separates consisting of bright blue denim fishing slacks worn with a crisp white cotton shirt and Huckleberry Finn straw hat were typical of McCardell's easy functionality in the 1940s and 1950s.

**ABOVE RIGHT:** Pared down Ready-to-Wear, produced in good quality natural fabrics became McCardell's signature style for modern women.

to complete the orders, and McCardell lost her job.

After a two-year stint working for designer Hattie Carnegie, she returned to a newly funded Townley Frocks in 1940 to launch her own line, Claire McCardell Clothes by Townley. Her original ideas included double topstitching only previously used in denim jeans; the 'popover dress', an unstructured wraparound dress with a visible metal stud fastening at one side; shoestring ties on sundresses; a one-piece romper bathing suit; leotards; and hoods. She was also responsible for the craze for flat pumps, requesting from the dancewear company Capezio that they add

# CLARE McCARDELL

leather soles to their ballet shoes, so they could be worn on the street.

McCardell was made a partner at Townley Frocks in 1952. In 1955, she was considered such a pioneer in the emergence of a new American style that she was pictured on the front cover of *Time* magazine, surrounded by models showcasing her winning designs – the romper suit, the dirndl skirt and the popover dress. In the same year, she was chosen to design a collection of dresses and separates using mass-produced fabric that had been created using prints taken from the work of some of the great French artists. The collaboration, instigated by the president of Fuller Fabrics, was much celebrated when it was launched as an exhibition and a *Life* editorial called 'Modern Art in Fashion', since McCardell's understated aesthetic perfectly suited the whimsical patterns of Picasso, Miró and Chagall.

Like Chanel before her, McCardell continually sought to improve the quality of life for a generation of increasingly independent women who wanted clothes to complement their active lifestyles. She incorporated functional elements into her designs, using zippers and metal press studs that were easy to fasten in a hurry and big patch pockets that looked stylish but were also highly practical. Basic fabrics like denim, mattress ticking, gingham and seersucker all achieved high fashion status in her hands, the ethos of usefulness over decorative embellishment a recurring theme. Despite her premature death at the age of 52, her legacy as one of the most influential designers in America continues.

**OPPOSITE:** Easy to wear cotton sun dresses and separates influenced by sportswear and produced in the graph paper check fabric that became synonymous with McCardell.

**RIGHT:** Ultra-modern crop tops and leotards were designed as beachwear as leisure activities became more popular in the USA in the late 1940s.

# PIERRE CARDIN

**SAN BIAGIO DI CALLALTA, ITALY**
1922–2020

**HIGHLIGHTS**
Sculptural geometric shapes for men and women, The Beatles' collarless jackets, patent leather boots.

**DESIGN ETHOS**
Inventive curiosity that embraced innovation in cultural art forms as well as fashion.

THE VISIONARY FRENCH DESIGNER PIERRE CARDIN CAN CLAIM MANY 'FIRSTS' IN A LONG AND SUCCESSFUL CAREER, BUT THE TALENTED MODERNIST (WHO WAS STILL WORKING AT THE AGE OF 95) IS MOST SYNONYMOUS WITH A PERIOD IN THE 1960S WHEN THE WHOLE WORLD SEEMED PREOCCUPIED WITH THE CONQUEST OF SPACE.

**BELOW:** Debonair Frenchman Pierre Cardin.

Cardin released his ground-breaking 'Cosmos' range in 1966, a pared-down collection of separates that included tabard-style tunics worn over ribbed tights, collarless jackets that zipped neatly to the neck, low-slung pants with zip-up patch pockets, bonnet felt hats and slim tank top-style vests with sculptural rolled necklines. The mix-and-match collection, produced in bold block colours, also included childrenswear in scaled-down replicas.

Cardin's approach to fashion was architectural, often taking inspiration from buildings and geometric shapes rather than the female form. 'I think of the dress, the woman doesn't matter,' he once said, and his interests in conceptual design extended to furniture, interiors, cars and buildings. A man of many exceptional talents, he was a pioneer in licensing, and during a career that spanned seven decades his logo was branded on to more than 800 products in 140 countries, making him one of the wealthiest men in France.

**ABOVE:** An extravagant evening gown from 1958; luxurious silk faille sheath dress with a decorative rose used to secure the voluminous open fronted overskirt.

# PIERRE CARDIN

**LEFT:** Space age modernity influenced many collections. Cardin favoured white wool gaberdine, and his white felt welders helmet became a defining image of the era.

**OPPOSITE:** Super short leather mini skirt with large metal eyelets worn with chunky metal jewellery in the form of a neckband and tie, 1969.

His childhood was not so affluent, though. Pierre Cardin was the youngest of 11 children, born to parents who worked in the vineyards in northern Italy before the family resettled in Saint-Étienne in southeast France. At the age of 17, he was apprenticed to a tailor in Vichy, where he stayed for several years before moving on to work for short periods for both Jeanne Paquin and Elsa Schiaparelli. Cardin was introduced to Christian Dior by Jean Cocteau (having helped make costumes for his 1946 film *La Belle et la Bête*) and was employed in his atelier as a cutter for suits and coats in time to be involved with his groundbreaking 'New Look' collection.

Cardin went on to establish his own couture house, producing elegant tailored collections in keeping with the feminine aesthetic of the day. Early output proved successful enough for him to quickly move to bigger premises in the 1st arrondissement, taking over a mansion on Rue du Faubourg Saint-Honoré in 1953, where he built a reputation for definitive clean-cut shapes that often surprised with one standout detail: giant buttons centred on a neat belted jacket, or an oversized shawl collar that encased the shoulders on a knitted mohair coat. A notable design was his spherical 'Bubble' dress in 1954, which then developed into the 'Balloon' coat dress (flared out and pulled back in with a drawstring running through the hem) and the pannier-shaped 'Puffball' cocktail dresses of the early 1960s.

Cardin was a pioneer in embracing diversity on the catwalk; following a trip to Tokyo, he brought back the first Japanese model who worked in Paris. Doll-sized Hiroko Matsumoto became his long-time muse, looking otherworldly in his stark futuristic shift dresses and helmet-like felt hats. His interest in democratizing fashion led to him selling a ready-to-wear collection through the French department store Le Printemps, flouting the strict conditions of the Chambre Syndicale de la Couture, who expelled him for the misdemeanour.

His interest in shape, structure and experimental materials remained a constant; he designed heavy denier-patterned tights to complement his mini shifts, stark metal body jewellery, thigh-high patent boots and vinyl bathing suits, and invented his own material, called Cardine – a synthetic fabric that was moulded to produce a three-dimensional pattern.

Worldwide fame and unlimited wealth came from licensing deals, putting his name on to a multitude of products not necessarily connected to fashion: sardines, matches, frying pans, pickle jars. He was criticized for such blatant commercialism, but Cardin was unmoved; a brilliant creative, he remained working until the end.

# PIERRE CARDIN

# OSSIE CLARK

**LIVERPOOL, ENGLAND**
1942–1996

**HIGHLIGHTS**
Quilted op art coat, chiffon gypsy dresses with handkerchief hems, python skin motorcycle jacket.

**DESIGN ETHOS**
Bohemian fantasy infused with rock star glamour for beautiful people.

ONE OF THE MOST INFLUENTIAL BRITISH DESIGNERS OF THE LATE 1960S AND EARLY '70S, OSSIE CLARK WAS AS FAMOUS AS THE ROCK STARS, CELEBRITIES AND MODELS HE DRESSED IN THE HEYDAY OF SWINGING LONDON.

Rejecting the industry's fascination with futurism, exemplified through the shiny plastics and short A-line modernity that dominated fashion at the start of the decade, Clark, in collaboration with his textile designer wife Celia Birtwell, looked backwards to a different era.

Taking inspiration from the 1930s and the skillful bias-cutting techniques of the great couturiers Madame Grès and Madeleine Vionnet, he pioneered a seismic change of mood and direction. *Vogue*'s 'New Ideas' editorial celebrated 'The Wizard of Ossie' with a four-page feature showing ruffled organdie shirts, crêpe skirts, tasselled sleeves and flared trousers. 'He's a magician leading a magical mysterious change of fashion now,' wrote fashion editor Marit Allen in 1968. Birtwell's lively prints on sensuous fabrics seamlessly mixed disparate patterns: panels of florals, checkerboards, spots, stars and stripes provided the perfect starting point for Clark's seductive collections designed to flatter women's bodies. Yet his satin trouser suits, voluminous-sleeved shirts and skinny 'Torpedo' scarves, originally designed for women, were equally embraced by a Chelsea crowd of hip young men, encouraged by flamboyant rock stars who flaunted their sexual ambiguity through a riot of print and colour.

Working under the brand name Quorum (with designer Alice Pollock and Birtwell), Clark's creative genius became increasingly authoritative; in 1966, he designed zip-up rocker jackets in leather that

# OSSIE CLARK

**ABOVE:** Ossie Clark in his Chelsea studio in London, 1968.

**OPPOSITE:** Feminine day dress with floaty sleeves, made up in viscose for Radley. Scattered daisies and delicate diagonal line print by Celia Birtwell are used as a single all-over pattern.

**LEFT:** Embracing the imaginative designs and vibrant colour of Birtwell's prints, (this one called 'Target' and inspired by the Ballet Russes), Clark excelled in cutting feminine shapes that offered an alternative to the space age 1960s aesthetic. This iconic photograph was taken by famed fashion photographer Jim Lee.

were copied by European designers the following year. His Quorum boutique in Chelsea was the epicentre of 'Happening' London, the destination for models, musicians and beautiful people who wanted to be seen wearing ground-breaking Ossie Clark designs; newspaper headlines hailed him 'The King of the King's Road'.

Christened Raymond Clark, the youngest of six children born into a large working-class family from Liverpool, the nickname Ossie originated when the family were evacuated to the Lancashire village of Oswaldtwistle during World War II. He inherited an abundance of style from his mother, who was a terrific knitter with a strong sense of colour, and by the age of 12 a young Ossie was making clothes for his extended family. Accepted into Manchester School of Art without a portfolio, based on just a few drawings of ballet dancers and Diana Vreeland-inspired fashion pieces that had been featured in *Harper's Bazaar*, Clark was given the opportunity of work experience and in 1960 he was sent to Christian Dior to soak up the rarefied atmosphere of the most successful couture house in Paris. Later, having won a scholarship to study fashion design at the Royal College of Art in London, Clark perfected his cutting skills and graduated in 1965 with a first-class honours degree and a feature in *Vogue* magazine that highlighted up-and-coming talent.

Clark's bohemian hippy style, which combined femininity and sex appeal, brought him great success, but demand was not only for the floaty chiffon dresses and wispy wide-legged culottes, made magical by hand-stitched embroidery and Birtwell's imaginative prints. His zip-up shortie leather jackets – made from panels of python snakeskin and pearlized and metallic leather, cut to cling to the body – presented a different aesthetic, as did the skintight leather jumpsuit held together with complicated laces that was designed specifically for his friend Mick Jagger. In 1972, Clark provided the stage clothes for Jagger's tour with the Rolling Stones, featuring

# OSSIE CLARK

a blue velvet all-in-one jumpsuit decorated with shiny silver circles that would glitter on stage, and a skintight white jumpsuit that unzipped from neck to groin, designed to reveal Jagger's famous torso.

By the mid-1970s, though, Clark was struggling. A tougher attitude in fashion prevailed with the subversive arrival of punk; there were money problems and legal wranglings with the company; and Celia had left him. Clark continued to make attempts at a comeback and kept going with one-off commissions for friends who remained loyal customers, until his tragic death at the age of 54. His visionary talent is acknowledged by a younger generation of designers who have been greatly influenced by his work.

**OPPOSITE:** Empire line chiffon day dress for Radley, with Birtwell's multi floral prints in bold colours inspired by her love of gardening.

**LEFT:** Sensual femininity came in the form of layers, ruffles and frills as part of the 'Ossie Clark Collection' from the early 1970s.

# MARY QUANT

**LONDON, ENGLAND**
1930–2023

**HIGHLIGHTS**
The miniskirt, hot pants, dropped-waist tunics, Black Cherry lipstick.

**DESIGN ETHOS**
Fun, ready-to-wear collections for a young clientele, that included underwear, shoes and make-up.

AS MUCH A PART OF THE SWINGING SIXTIES AS POP ART AND THE BEATLES, MARY QUANT WAS CREDITED WITH CHANGING THE FACE OF FASHION WITH THE INVENTION OF THE MINISKIRT.

**ABOVE:** Mary Quant with the author Emma Baxter-Wright on a fashion shoot in 1990.

**OPPOSITE:** One of the first to diversify into a full range of youthful accessories, Quant produced shoes in every shade in 1972 to complement her clothing range.

Her innovative designs fizzed with vitality, in a decade that saw a revolution of young people pushing against the establishment, in every area of creativity. Tiny hot pants, dropped-waist pinafore dresses, PVC rain macs, patterned tights and a stylish make-up range that embraced the dazzling colours she championed for her clothes were just some of her modern ideas.

Her first boutique, Bazaar, opened on the King's Road in London in October 1955 and provided a collection of bright, easy-to-wear pieces that appealed to a burgeoning market of fashion-conscious teenagers determined to break away from the drab post-war respectability of their mothers' wardrobes. Initially buying fabric from the haberdashery department at Harrods and running up clothes on a sewing machine in her bedsit, Quant and Bazaar saw almost immediate success. For the first time in history, young women had a pay packet that allowed them to choose outfits that were sexy, practical and fun. Quant's playful pieces reflected her customers' newfound emancipation. 'Snobbery has gone out of fashion. The things I was making had nothing to do with accepted couture,' she wrote in her 1966 biography *Quant by Quant* (Cassel & Co.). Modelling her own designs, Quant became the fashionable figurehead of her 'Chelsea Look', instantly recognized by her sharp Sassoon bob, micro-mini and knee-high wet-look boots.

# MARY QUANT

**ABOVE:** American model Kellie Wilson photographed by Duffy wearing a 1966 design for The Ginger Group. Quant designed the matching shorts to go with the minidress because she had noticed girls in short shirts were 'kicking their legs around more than before and the results weren't always attractive'.

At 16, desperate to escape suburbia, a decision to go to Goldsmiths School of Art changed the direction of Quant's life. Although her schoolteacher parents refused to let her study fashion, Quant embarked on an art diploma course, and at Goldsmiths she met and fell in love with Alexander Plunket Greene, who became her husband and lifelong business partner. Her first job working for Erik, a couture milliner in Brook Street, convinced her that bespoke fashion, which was prohibitively expensive and elitist (it took three days to produce a hat for a client), was totally inappropriate for her generation. Financially backed by her boyfriend and a friend, Archie McNair, the trio opened a King's Road boutique that sold unusual accessories and jewellery sourced from the London art schools, plus a few original pieces Quant had made herself.

Bazaar quickly became a hot spot for young Londoners as Quant added more of her own designs; her ethos that 'clothes should live, breathe and move with the wearer' proved to be a winning formula. She took evening classes on cutting, adapted ideas from Butterick paper patterns and hired a couple of dressmakers to run up the simple sporty shapes she was designing. Mass production became inevitable and in 1963 she launched the Ginger Group to manufacture her wholesale designs. Quant was astute in recognizing the changing world she was a part of; her catwalk shows were staged as parties, with girls dancing down the runway to loud pop music while sipping champagne; she commissioned long-legged mannequins that looked like Jean Shrimpton for the shop windows; and her affordable clothes celebrated vibrant colour, often clashing spots and stripes, and utilized new advancements in fabric technology.

Within ten years, Mary Quant had achieved global success, her distinctive daisy logo a recognized symbol of the brand. A complete make-up and skincare range was launched in 1966 and she later agreed licensing deals to manufacture shoes, sunglasses, bed linen and alcohol. With a commercial range for the American department store JCPenney, she became an international star, and was awarded both an OBE (1966) and a CBE (2022) for her outstanding contribution to British fashion and culture.

# MARY QUANT

**OPPOSITE TOP:** Strong colour and simple shapes, like this unstructured wool shift dress from 2003 remained a constant Quant signature throughout her career.

**OPPOSITE BELOW:** Designing the total look, with matching PVC raincoats, wellington boots and rain hats from Mary Quant's 'Wet Collection'.

**ABOVE:** Quant working in Paris in 2004; her famous daisy motif appeared on every product from swimsuits to make-up palettes.

67

# PACO RABANNE

**SAN SEBASTIÁN, SPAIN** 1934–2023

**HIGHLIGHTS**
Space age metal shift dresses, body armour jewellery, paper dresses.

**DESIGN ETHOS**
Futuristic fashion using unconventional industrial materials.

## IN THE MID-1960S, INSPIRED BY THE SPACE RACE, FASHION TOOK A FUTURISTIC TURN, GLEANING MOTIVATION FROM ALL THINGS COSMIC.

**ABOVE:** Paco Rabanne in his atelier workshop, wielding a wooden carpenter's mallet.

**OPPOSITE:** Clothes were often constructed as opposed to stitched, favouring unusual materials like this silver lamé thread, knitted into a tabard mini, and patchwork leather gilet held together with metal eyelets, 1967.

Geometric haircuts and space age bonnets pervaded the catwalk collections, and Paco Rabanne (who had originally trained as an architect) pushed the concept of New Age design further than anyone, making a name for himself as a radical creative.

His revolutionary ideas on the runway confounded the fashion press, his choice of unorthodox materials and new shapes a daring departure from the expected elegance of Parisian design. Working with new forms of technological advancements in materials, Rabanne, who favoured the term 'engineer' over 'designer', experimented with Rhodoid plastics, crinkled paper, metal discs and fluid chain mail. His extraordinary vision of ultra-modern clothes produced items that were 'assembled' rather than traditionally stitched. Flat plastic buttons were stapled together to make rudimentary A-line shifts, worn over flesh-coloured body stockings, and he was often photographed wielding a signature pair of pliers, used to make adjustments to minidresses strung together with wire and metal rings. 'Who cares if no one can wear my dresses,' he said. 'They are statements.'

With a mother who worked as a couture seamstress for Cristóbal Balenciaga, Paco Rabanne was immersed in the fashion industry from an early age. In his twenties, he chose architecture as a career and studied at the École des Beaux-Arts in Paris for a decade, making money to pay for his education by sketching ideas for handbags and selling them to established fashion designers. This ignited a short-lived career designing bold-shaped buttons, jewellery

# PACO RABANNE

and accessories in modern pliable plastics, which he sold to the prestigious couture houses of Christian Dior and Hubert de Givenchy.

His debut collection in 1964, called 'Twelve Experimental Dresses', set the aesthetic tone for what was to come, with the designer clearly elevating dynamic impact over practicality and comfort. The craft-based skills utilized in his jewellery creations were transposed to entire outfits, and two years later he presented 'Twelve Unwearable Dresses in Contemporary Materials' at the Hotel George V in Paris. Producing an effect akin to modern chain mail, his sculptural mini tunics were constructed entirely from squares and rectangles of thin aluminium plates of various sizes, held together at the corners with metal rings. Other 'fabric' was created from iridescent plastic discs joined by metal jump rings, producing surprisingly lightweight shift dresses that were designed to be worn over a naked body. Semi-transparent clothes and suggestive glimpses of nudity were fashionable tropes in the 1960s, and with commentators either outraged or enchanted at the

# PACO RABANNE

audacity of his vision, worldwide fame was secured. Vocal support came from authoritative Americans, such as Diana Vreeland and Peggy Guggenheim, who championed his imaginative use of industrial materials. Scott Paper, the American toilet paper company, also helped, with a commission to design a range of throwaway paper dresses alongside his metal creations.

Innovation continued with the introduction of diamonds, mirrored paillettes and gold into the commercial world of high fashion, and although Rabanne retired from his own house in 1999, the brand name survived with a range of successful fragrances. As a designer committed to exploration, Paco Rabanne remains highly influential to a modern generation of designers.

**ABOVE:** Showcasing a sculptural aesthetic for his Autumn/Winter haute couture collection in Paris, 1985.

**OPPOSITE:** Models wearing a collection of Rabanne's chain metal dresses on the French television show *Dim Dam Dom*, early 1970's.

# YVES SAINT LAURENT

**ORAN, ALGERIA**
1936–2008

**HIGHLIGHTS**
'Le Smoking' trouser suit, Mondrian dress, transparent blouse, safari suit, ready-to-wear clothes for both sexes, retailed through the Rive Gauche boutiques.

**DESIGN ETHOS**
Fashion inspiration taken from global culture, travel, ballet, theatre and art.

KNOWN FOR BOTH HIS PRODIGIOUS TALENT AND FRAGILE PERSONALITY, YVES SAINT LAURENT WAS WIDELY ACCLAIMED IN HIS LIFETIME, ALONGSIDE DIOR AND CHANEL, AS ONE OF THE GREATEST COUTURIERS OF THE 20TH CENTURY.

His career successfully straddled two distinct periods in fashion, both of which shaped his *oeuvre*. These ranged from the specific demands of elegant 1950s couture to the street styles his ready-to-wear collections championed in subsequent decades, and both proved beneficial to his legacy. Many of his brilliant fashion innovations, such as the double-breasted pea coat, pussycat bow blouse and tailored trouser suit, still resonate as modern classics.

In 1954, a painfully shy young man from Algeria stepped into the fashion spotlight in Paris to claim first prize in a prestigious design competition judged by Hubert de Givenchy. Early recognition of Yves Saint Laurent's talent secured him a job learning the complex procedures of couture within the best house in Paris, alongside Christian Dior. Working as his assistant, many of Saint Laurent's designs were chosen to be included in Dior's presentations, but the apprenticeship ended abruptly just three years later when Dior died unexpectedly. His 21-year-old protégé was chosen to take over as the creative director of the house and won rave reviews for his debut 1957 'Trapeze' collection, with headlines declaring, 'Saint Laurent has saved France'. Less well received was the jazz-influenced 1960 'Beat' collection, featuring black crocodile skin jackets with mink trims, designs that proved too unorthodox for the cautiously conservative clientele.

When Saint Laurent was called up to fight in the Algerian colonial war, the billionaire owner of Dior did not contest the draft papers. On Saint Laurent's release from a military hospital, he discovered that his

# YVES SAINT LAURENT

**OPPOSITE:** The original Mondrian dresses from the Autumn/Winter 1965 collection were revived as 'classics' throughout Saint Laurent's long career.

**ABOVE:** Yves Saint Laurent with Betty Catroux (left) and Loulou de la Falaise, at the opening of his London Rive Gauche boutique in 1969, all wearing his new unisex khaki cotton jacket.

**RIGHT:** A totally sheer evening dress from 1968, with a trim of ostrich feathers around the hips to maintain modesty.

# YVES SAINT LAURENT

**OPPOSITE:** 'Le Smoking' worn with mannish trousers became a signature for YSL re-examined thoroughout his 40 years at the top. It is shown here at his retrospective show at the Centre Georges Pompidou, 2002.

**RIGHT:** Saint Laurent's twice-yearly catwalk shows became the highlight of Paris fashion week, astonishing the audience with vibrant colour, lavish fabrics and exquisite levels of craftsmanship, Spring/Summer 1993.

position at Dior had been filled, so together with his business partner Pierre Bergé, he launched his own label, presenting the first Yves Saint Laurent collection in January 1962.

Socializing with a hip young crowd in Paris, new ideas, shaped by the changes in society and female liberation, tumbled out of the pages of his sketch books and on to the runway. Functional modernism in the form of short shift dresses, wide-legged pants and double-breasted sailor coats were all hailed as great successes within the first few seasons, and the geometric colour block dresses inspired by the Dutch artist Piet Mondrian sealed Saint Laurent's global reputation as the most exciting couturier in Paris.

Indeed, Saint Laurent's love affair with art provided multiple opportunities throughout his career to reinterpret works on canvas into sublime expressions of beauty on the body. Pop art, cubism and impressionism were all transposed from artworks into fashion, utilizing bold colour palettes and exquisite hand-crafted embroidery. In 1966, flanked by best friends Catherine Deneuve and Betty Catroux, Saint Laurent opened the first Rive Gauche boutique in Saint-Germain, Paris. The concept store of ready-to-wear items included suede miniskirts, trouser suits, knitted minidresses and chunky silver jewellery, all pitched at prices that a young customer could afford. His tuxedo trouser suits, 'Le Smoking', designed for women, became a house staple that would be updated and reinterpreted in every future collection.

Posing naked in 1971 for the advertising campaign for his first menswear fragrance, Pour Homme, caused a terrific scandal for Saint Laurent, while boosting sales. More controversy was to come with the provocative launch of the perfume Opium, with the accompanying strapline: 'for those who are addicted to Yves Saint Laurent'.

The house aesthetic became increasingly lavish in the late 1970s and '80s as Saint Laurent consolidated his fantasy vision of global culture, conceived from the comfort of his own sofa. Russia, Spain, Imperial China and India were all given a theatrical make-over, presented on a catwalk at the Hotel InterContinental in Paris for the first time, with a booming operatic soundtrack, each collection more dazzlingly colourful and opulent than the last.

Yves Saint Laurent suffered from ill health all his life and retired from a sensational 40-year career in 2002. His outstanding legacy is celebrated in two museums, one in Paris and the other in Marrakesh, which showcase hundreds of his couture pieces.

75

**DES MOINES, IOWA, USA**

1932–1990

**HIGHLIGHTS**
Halter neck jumpsuits, Ultrasuede shirt dresses, kaftans.

**DESIGN ETHOS**
Fluid, understated minimalism to create maximum sex appeal.

# HALSTON

TALL, GOOD-LOOKING AND AN INTEGRAL PART OF THE GLAMOROUS STUDIO 54 NEW YORK JET SET, HALSTON WAS INTERNATIONALLY ACKNOWLEDGED AS THE LABEL EVERYBODY WANTED TO BE SEEN IN, NAMED BY *NEWSWEEK* MAGAZINE IN 1972 AS 'THE PREMIER FASHION DESIGNER OF ALL AMERICA'.

**BELOW:** Roy Halston Frowick started his career as a milliner, seen here with Italian movie star Virna Lisi.

His modern, sexy aesthetic dominated the decade, characterized by clothes that spurned tailored structure and concentrated instead on sensual fluidity. His face became as famous as the stars he dressed and was seen socializing with – Elizabeth Taylor, Liza Minelli, Ali MacGraw and Bianca Jagger all adored his pared-down luxury that eschewed decorative details in favour of elegant simplicity.

Halston excelled in producing loose, comfortable clothes, using silk jersey fabrics and soft cashmere knits that draped softly around the body. His trademark timeless pieces included tie-dye chiffon pyjama suits with plunging necklines, matte jersey wrap skirts, kaftans worn over loose chiffon trousers and narrow body-skimming evening dresses with halter neck ties or one-shoulder asymmetric designs. In the early 1970s, the Ultrasuede shirt dress he created, inspired by a man's long-sleeved work shirt and made from Ultrasuede, a new synthetic mix of machine-washable fabric that resembled authentic suede, became a worldwide bestseller as the go-to sporty staple every modern woman needed.

An interest in fashion and, more specifically, a talent for creating contemporary millinery was evident from an early age in Roy Halston Frowick, who grew up in a chaotic family in Midwestern America. As a

# HALSTON

**LEFT:** Halston became a New York superstar, socializing with the cool 'in crowd' including artist Andy Warhol.

**BELOW:** Clean simple lines, expert cutting using slinky fabrics and block colour, typified the Halston look in the 1970s, modelled by Anjelica Huston in 1972.

teenager at school, his classmates remembered he was always dressed in his own impeccable style (later, he rarely strayed from his relaxed 'uniform' of slim pants, a cashmere turtleneck and an Ultrasuede jacket). A short stint at Indiana University was abandoned in favour of evening courses at the Art Institute of Chicago, where he also had a burgeoning sideline creating hats for wealthy customers booked into the city's premier hair salon at the Ambassador Hotel. This led to a move to New York City, initially to work for Madame Lilly Daché, a renowned milliner who operated from an apartment off Park Avenue, and then in 1959 to the millinery department in the upmarket retail store Bergdorf Goodman. It was here that he designed the pale-blue pillbox hat that Jackie Kennedy wore in 1961 on the day of her husband's presidential inauguration.

Aware that millinery was becoming less fashionable, Halston persuaded Bergdorf Goodman to sponsor his first ready-to-wear collection in 1966, and two years later he set up his own business catering to a prestigious clientele. Fame and success came quickly, and within a few years he had won his third Coty Award (the highest honour in the American fashion industry) and the sleek, fluid lines that had become his signature chimed perfectly with the sexy

**RIGHT:** Liza Minelli in fluid sequin evening dress with plunging neckline and matching coat, arriving at the Versailles fashion extravaganza in 1973.

**OPPOSITE:** Asymmetric evening dress in deep purple satin, 1981, with oversized tie at the shoulder, flowing train and high split seams.

sophistication of the 1970s New York disco scene. His vision of laid-back minimalism took cues from the tubular art deco-influenced 1930s; he presented narrow slip dresses that followed the female form, reworked fluid silk pyjama pants, and presented fine cashmere cardigans cut long over slim hips. His streamlined silhouette eliminated complex seams and inner linings and kept all fastenings discreet.

Having found his forte, Halston spent years perfecting variations on the same elegant lines that had been so successful for him. He believed in the subtle evolution of design rather than constantly introducing new attention-grabbing ideas. By the early 1980s he had sold his name to Norton Simon Inc. and was increasingly involved with the business of licensing products. A deal with the giant retailer JCPenney to effectively democratize fashion and dress the mass market of America turned out to be a disaster, with his A-list clientele and upmarket retailers horrified to be associated with the same designer who was catering for the suburban housewife. Halston's reputation in later years was diminished by problems with addiction and the continued dilution of his brand name, which he tried unsuccessfully to buy back.

# HALSTON

# KENZŌ TAKADA

**HIMEJI, JAPAN**
1939–2020

**HIGHLIGHTS**
Mismatched print and stripes, smock tops, square-cut sweaters.

**DESIGN ETHOS**
Hybrid ethnicity that collages elements of traditional style from global sources.

## A RIOTOUS MIX OF COLOUR, PATTERN AND PRINT SIGNALLED THE ARRIVAL OF THE HOTTEST NEW BOUTIQUE IN PARIS IN 1970.

**ABOVE:** Kenzo Takada in his Parisian atelier.

**OPPOSITE:** Modern sportswear for Spring/Summer 1973, inspired by 1930s bathing suits.

Jungle Jap, a small shop in the grand Galerie Vivienne, was the brainchild of Japanese designer Kenzō Takada, who successfully cross-referenced a melting pot of cultural influences to conjure up his sensational 'ethnic look'. Inspired by the lush jungle paintings of naive artist Henri Rousseau, Takada painted his interior shop walls with murals that depicted exotic lotus flowers, reclining nudes and swaggering tigers stalking purposefully behind rain forest ferns.

With impeccable timing, his ready-to-wear boutique attracted an enthusiastic clientele of models and celebrities who were intrigued by the late '60s trend for hippy culture he was promoting. The shop resembled a multicoloured bazaar, with merchandise hung off traditional wooden coat stands and decoratively laid out on long, low tables. Pretty floral dresses mixed prints with patchwork quilting, elements of vintage Victoriana amalgamated with Eastern silhouettes and cutting techniques, skirts wrapped around the body and trousers were fluid and wide-legged. With a masterful eye, Takada's innovative styling ideas mixed up global references with his inherent Japanese heritage, creating a sophisticated vision of colourful nonconformity that proved very desirable. The brand name was quickly changed from Jungle Jap to Kenzō but the hybrid aesthetic remained, and in 2019, looking back on his career. Takada told the *Financial Times*, 'By the end of the 1970s Kenzō was the number one selling brand worldwide.'

Despite an early interest in fashion gleaned through the pages of his sister's fashion magazines,

# KENZŌ TAKADA

Takada's austere parents opposed the idea of their son having any sort of creative career, so instead he enrolled at Kobe University to study literature. By 1958, he had dropped out and switched paths. As one of the first male students to study at the Bunka Fashion College in Tokyo, his promising talent was recognized, and he won the 1960 So-En award and soon after began designing childrenswear for the department store Sanai.

Determined to get to Paris, Takada used financial compensation from the government, who had bulldozed his flat to make preparations for the 1964 Tokyo Olympics, to buy a ticket. The eight-week journey by boat took him via Hong Kong (China), Colombo, Egypt, Spain and Marseilles and he arrived as a lonely outsider in Paris where he earned a modest living selling 25-franc fashion sketches to design houses including Louis Féraud, all the while scouring the flea markets searching out unusual fabrics that could be turned into garments for his first collection.

From his Parisian debut in 1970, Takada's imaginative style made a dynamic fashion statement that upended the established face of French fashion. An early trip home kick-started the idea of knitwear based on the square-cut shapes of the kimono, which was easy to wear but also elegant, and this boxy basic-shaped knit became a signature piece, albeit in vibrant mismatched stripes and clashing blocks of colour. His fun-filled shows were theatrical affairs; in 1978, he presented from a circus tent, models competing for attention with trapeze artists, mingling with the orchestra and arriving in the big top on horseback. Takada himself stole the limelight, closing the show riding on the back of an elephant.

Referencing myriad different styles, often in the same outfit, Takada's message of global inclusivity was intrinsic in all he produced. He was also one of the first to embrace diversity on the catwalk, using models from all ethnicities and sending groups of happy models down the runway together to present a cohesive view of the collection.

In 1993, Takada sold his company to LVMH, where he stayed on for six years before announcing his retirement in 1999.

# KENZŌ TAKADA

**OPPOSITE ABOVE:** Bright colour and playful details including pom poms on the drawstring pants, from 1979.

**OPPOSITE BELOW:** Working from a dynamic colour palette, Kenzo often included colour matched accessories with his youthful collections of sporty separates, from the Autumn/Winter Ready-to-Wear show 1985.

**RIGHT:** A master of juxtaposing colour and print and successfully playing with scale, Kenzo mixes overblown florals with miniature blooms and decorative prints for Spring/Summer 1988.

# VALENTINO GARAVANI

**VOGHERA, ITALY** 1932–

**HIGHLIGHTS**
Fluid evening wear, Jacqueline Kennedy wedding dress, 'Valentino Red'.

**DESIGN ETHOS**
Classicism infused with glamour.

FOR OVER 60 YEARS, THE PERFECTLY COIFFED, PERMA-TANNED VALENTINO GARAVANI (SO FAMOUS HE USES ONLY HIS FIRST NAME) HAS BEEN KNOWN AS THE KING OF JET SET CHIC, CULTIVATING AN EFFORTLESSLY GLAMOROUS IMAGE OF HIMSELF ALONGSIDE THE BEAUTIFUL WOMEN HE DRESSES.

**BELOW:** Valentino Garavani with the influential US fashion journalist Diana Vreeland

**OPPOSITE LEFT:** Elegant evening dress with dramatic deep V neckline from the Ready-to-Wear collection Spring/Summer 1976.

**OPPOSITE RIGHT:** Figure-hugging dress, with signature ribbon bow at the neckline, modelled by Naomi Campbell from the Haute Couture collection 1992.

From Elizabeth Taylor, Audrey Hepburn and Jacqueline Kennedy in the 1960s and '70s to current red carpet stars Gwyneth Paltrow, Jennifer Aniston and Nicole Kidman, Valentino has survived and thrived at the top, utilizing his remarkable talent to remain relevant over the decades.

Valentino Clemente Ludovico Garavani was born in northern Italy, where as a child his early trips to the cinema introduced him to the glamorous stars of 1930s Hollywood, such as Judy Garland and Lana Turner. Captivated by their beautiful clothes, Valentino spent hours as a young teen sketching evening dresses, and in 1949 he enrolled at the Santa Maria Institute in Milan to study fashion illustration. Further studies at the École des Beaux-Arts in Paris led to an apprentice job at society couturier Jean Dessès, where he spent five years learning how to create couture evening wear. Alongside him was Guy Laroche, and when Laroche left to set up his own company in 1957, Valentino went with him, gaining invaluable experience in the day-to-day running of a fashion company.

Taking the knowledge he had learned in Paris and financially backed by his father, Valentino opened his first fashion business in Rome on the prestigious Via Condotti, in 1959. The grand dream was to emulate a Parisian couture house, so he only used the most

# VALENTINO GARAVANI

**LEFT:** Ultra feminine couture evening dress with pin tucked bodice and jewel and feather fringing sweeping across one shoulder, 2007.

**OPPOSITE:** Models on the catwalk applaud Valentino at the finale of his Spring/Summer Ready-to-Wear collection 2008, held at the 'Carousel du Louvre' Paris.

luxurious fabrics and had French models flown in from Paris to show his collections. A chance meeting with a young architecture student at the Café de Paris in Via Veneto changed the course of Valentino's life; his enduring relationship with Giancarlo Giammetti (the business brains behind the phenomenal success) turned Valentino himself and his empire into one of the wealthiest in the world of fashion.

Often described at Italy's greatest couturier, he won the respect of the hard-to-please Parisian fashion crowd through a commitment to exacting standards of beauty. His showstopping evening dresses, coveted by A-list stars and celebrities, champion Valentino's romantic fluidity and couture levels of craftsmanship, usually offset with a surprising flourish of ruffles, a gargantuan bow or lavish embroidery.

The overriding objective in all his creativity is a desire to make women look beautiful. 'Forget about fashion, the grunge look, the messy look. I cannot see women destroyed, uncombed or strange. I want to make a girl who arrives, and makes people turn and say "You look sensational",' he told *Vanity Fair* in 2004. As a teenager, a trip to see *La Traviata* at the opera house in Barcelona ignited a passion for the colour red, which Valentino developed into his own very particular shade of vermilion, now known as Valentino Red. It has become a signature for the house, included in every show since his very first collection in 1962. The impact of a woman dressed entirely in Valentino Red is hard to ignore.

Early publicity came when Elizabeth Taylor wore a Valentino gown for the premiere of *Spartacus* in 1960. The pictures were syndicated internationally, and the following day the most famous actress in the world chose seven other outfits from the salon, forming a lifelong friendship with the designer. Taylor's patronage encouraged others and soon Valentino had some of the world's most influential women added

# VALENTINO GARAVANI

to his client list: Babe Paley, Jacqueline de Ribes and Jackie Kennedy.

His all-white winter collection (Collezione 'Bianca') shown in Rome in 1968 was a triumph of restrained classicism. Ankle-length skirts cut to flatter the body were shown with neat tailored jackets and ladylike blouses decorated with pearl seeds and embroidery, and the white on white was the ultimate statement in luxury. The success of the Collezione 'Bianca' led to a commission to design Jackie Kennedy's wedding outfit, an ivory georgette and lace dress, when she married Aristotle Onassis on a Greek island in 1968.

Valentino's ability to sustain his position as the designer of choice for every successive generation of celebrities is unsurpassed, and his beautiful creations still dominate star-studded red-carpet occasions including the Met Ball and the Oscars. Valentino and Giancarlo sold their business twice within a five-year period in 1998 and 2002, with the influential designer remaining in charge both times.

Valentino presented his final Spring/Summer 2008 ready-to-wear show in Paris, surrounded for the finale by a troupe of supermodels wearing his iconic red evening dresses.

# YOHJI YAMAMOTO

**TOKYO, JAPAN**
1943–

**HIGHLIGHTS**
Red chiffon bustle, men's oversized unstructured suits, bamboo crinoline wedding dress.

**DESIGN ETHOS**
Androgyny achieved through deliberate disarray and thoughtful asymmetry.

WHEN AN UNKNOWN JAPANESE DESIGNER DEBUTED HIS COLLECTION AT PARIS FASHION WEEK IN 1981, THE ELITE AUDIENCE WERE VISIBLY CONFUSED BY A SHOW THAT WAS UNLIKE ANYTHING THEY HAD EVER SEEN BEFORE.

Yohji Yamamoto presented his revolutionary ideas with pale-faced waifs who walked to a stark soundtrack that amplified the thud of a human heartbeat. The show consisted mostly of black oversized garments that hung loosely off androgynous-looking models. The cuts were often asymmetric and without decorative embellishment. Pockets were positioned in strange places with a deliberate absence of either masculine or feminine features. Seams were visible on the outside, sometimes left unfinished with cotton threads spiralling down the fabric. Hemlines were intentionally uneven, there were conspicuous rips and holes everywhere, and this singular unsettling vision was only complemented by the addition of plain white shirts and flat shoes.

Fashionistas were disorientated by this radical presentation. An abundance of black was not considered an appropriate high fashion colour, the

**LEFT:** Yohji Yamamoto backstage in Paris 1989.

**OPPOSITE:** Black became Yamamoto's signature colour, occasionally offset with white or a flash of red, as here with Erin O'Connor's ruby wig, in 2000.

YOHJI YAMAMOTO

**LEFT:** Clever construction and a dramatic silhouette often exemplify each piece, as in this black dress with voluminous red bustle from Autumn/Winter 1986.

**OPPOSITE:** Yamamoto continually challenged the status quo of high fashion with revolutionary collections that could be worn by both sexes. Soft unstructured menswear shown here from 2005, ia perfect example of his unorthodox style.

term 'Hiroshima Chic' was mentioned, and French newspaper *Le Figaro* described 'A World War II survivor's look'. Others understood this unconventional collection to be the start of a new direction for fashion, an unveiling to a wider world of an aesthetic that Yamamoto had already been perfecting in Japan for the previous nine years.

The founding principles of Yohji's style have remained consistently intact for half a century, with only subtle changes and renewals. His long-standing career has achieved cult status and devotion from existing fans who embraced his exploratory view from the beginning and also a new generation of anti-fashion fans who reject blatant branding and logos. His signature colour continues overwhelmingly to be black, offset with white and the occasional flash of red, the only colour he thinks can compete with black. An intention to defuse overt sexuality in fashion by producing clothes that conceal rather than reveal is endlessly achieved by billowing shapes that fall softly around the body. 'It is not polite to other people to show off too much,' he told the *New York Times* when he started out, and an insistence that 'fabric is everything' means that the choice of textiles for an outfit is always the determining factor for the final silhouette.

Yamamoto trained to be a lawyer at Keio University in Tokyo but found the subject too boring to commit his life to. After

# YOHJI YAMAMOTO

completing his degree, he worked alongside his war-widowed mother, who made dresses to support her son, before signing up to study at Bunka Fashion College. Working first as a freelance designer, he went on to establish his own company, Y's Incorporated, in 1972 and presented his first 'Y' collection in Tokyo five years later. Breaking all existing fashion conventions and rejecting trends, Yamamoto arrived in Paris in the early 1980s with Rei Kawakubo, the Japanese duo taking the capital by storm with their shared ideas of modern deconstructionist clothing. His starting point has always been to put women into what were traditionally considered men's garments, to design pieces that provide a layer of protection for women – from cold weather, but also from the male gaze. The mainstay of his collections – functional workwear and soft oversized suits (for both sexes) – are designed to last a long time, intentionally made from strong fabrics that look and feel better with the ageing process. The strongest motivation for Yamamoto, who is often celebrated as an intellectual fashion purist, is not how the clothes look on the body, but how they make the person feel.

In 2002, the Y-3 collaboration with Adidas was launched. Yamamoto was the first designer (and many others have followed his lead) to create a range of trainers and sportswear that successfully fused high-end performance sportswear with his unique avant-garde aesthetic. 'I never follow rules. I like to break them,' he said in a recent interview for *W* magazine. In reality, Yamamoto, who has become a living legend, has built a career following his own directives, searching out the personal relationship between clothes and the human body and creating great beauty from imperfection.

# STEPHEN SPROUSE

**DAYTON, OHIO, USA** 1953–2004

**HIGHLIGHTS**
Sequin trapeze dresses, Day-Glo graffiti, asymmetric dresses for Debbie Harry.

**DESIGN ETHOS**
Clean-cut modernism heavily influenced by a post-punk aesthetic.

GRAVITATING AWAY FROM AN APPRENTICESHIP IN THE GENTRIFIED WORLD OF HIGH FASHION, STEPHEN SPROUSE WAS DECLARED THE COOLEST DESIGNER IN NEW YORK CITY IN THE EARLY 1980S.

Imbued with skinny rock star nonchalance, he would hang out at the downtown Mudd Club with a crowd of like-minded musicians and artists who inspired his take on fashion futurism. Merging the dark-edged nihilism of punk with an acid colour palette, Sprouse created his own new wave of modern glamour, which stylistically owed much to the 1960s – his favourite period of fashion – but that he stamped distinctly as his own. With Blondie's Debbie Harry as his flatmate and the striking transexual model Teri Toye as his muse, Strouse had acquired two dazzling peroxide blondes to showcase his outfits.

Having previously worked for Halston and gained experience of the luxury market, Sprouse rejected the elitism of uptown society in favour of a more bohemian crowd. An avid sketcher who was rarely seen without a pen in his hand, he was inspired by the slogans scrawled across punk clothing and the subway art of Keith Haring and Jean-Michel Basquiat, both of whom utilized graphic texts in their work. His handwritten graffiti print applied on vibrant cut-out jersey shift dresses and sequin miniskirts in 1984 immediately became a successful signature. When Marc Jacobs commissioned Sprouse to graffiti over the famous LV monogram in 2001, the collaboration on luggage and handbags became an instant hit, with long waiting lists to acquire the cult items.

Sprouse grew up in Columbus, Indiana, where his formative years were spent creating pictures that emulated the artworks of his heroes, Frank Stella and

# STEPHEN SPROUSE

Andy Warhol. Both of Sprouse's parents were supportive of his talent, sending his detailed fashion drawings to Dorothy Fuller, a fashion visionary at the Art Institute of Chicago, which led to a summer internship with Bill Blass. At the age of 18, he briefly attended the Rhode Island School of Design but left to take a job with Roy Halston Fenwick. For two years, Sprouse lived a dual

**OPPOSITE:** Stephen Sprouse embracing model Kate Moss in the early 1990s.

**ABOVE:** Debbie Harry from fabled pop group Blondie was the perfect poster girl for Sprouse, and wore his designs on and off stage.

# STEPHEN SPROUSE

**OPPOSITE:** Acid brights defined the Sprouse colour palette, body hugging sequins and oversized puffa jacket from Autumn/Winter 1998

**RIGHT:** Inspired by the classic shift mini dresses of the 1960's, Sprouse embellished his day glo colours with black graffiti and abstract psychedelic patterns.

existence, working long hours for Halston surrounded by Fifth Avenue socialites and rubbing shoulders with his idols Andy Warhol and Barbra Streisand, while simultaneously living downtown in a Bowery loft with an arty crowd of up-and-coming creatives who would socialize at legendary music club CBGB.

In 1982, some of Sprouse's early designs were included in a show of emerging talent alongside those of Anna Sui and Vivienne Tam. Disappointed that Keith Haring could not collaborate with him on print ideas for his clothes (he was under contract to Vivienne Westwood), Sprouse developed a personal style of writing powerful graphic text across his clothes, creating a visual immediacy that looked sharp and fresh. Keeping silhouettes stark, he played with lurid newspaper headlines and images, blown up on a colour Xerox machine, that were then distorted across T-shirts, pants and dresses.

In 1983, he launched his own label with a show that merged rock 'n roll and inner-city street style, including Day-Glo trapeze-shaped shifts in contrasting colours, silk micro-minis with the word 'LOVE' spray-painted across the body, graffitied leggings, motorcycle boots and silver jewellery in the shape of alphabet letters. Subsequent shows took inspiration from space, showing silver leather coats bearing satellite photographs from NASA that were used to create interplanetary prints.

His label gained a cult following, but despite industry recognition as Best New Designer in 1984 and huge commercial success for the collections that followed, he struggled financially, and his stores closed in 1989. There were many attempts at new starts: the Andy Warhol Foundation for the Visual Arts gave Sprouse exclusive rights to use his imagery for clothes; he was commissioned to design capsule collections for Bergdorf Goodman and Barneys; and he designed stage costumes for Axl Rose, Duran Duran and Billy Idol. The Louis Vuitton collaboration in 2001 reinvigorated his name and introduced him to a new generation of fashion lovers. In the three years before his death, Sprouse was in demand again, working on projects for Diesel, Target and BMW.

# KATHARINE HAMNETT

**KENT, ENGLAND**
1947–

**HIGHLIGHTS**
Slogan T-shirts, boiler suits, RAF-style bomber jackets made from crumpled parachute silk.

**DESIGN ETHOS**
Political activist and environmentalist who turned campaigning T-shirts into high fashion.

IF A DECADE CAN BE DEFINED BY ONE ICONIC FASHION SCENE, THEN KATHARINE HAMNETT CONFRONTING A STONY-FACED MARGARET THATCHER AT A DOWNING STREET FASHION WEEK RECEPTION IN 1984 ENCAPSULATED THAT MOMENT.

**ABOVE:** Katharine Hamnett famously confronting prime minister Margaret Thatcher at a Downing Street reception in her '58% Don't Want Pershing' T-shirt dress in 1984.

**OPPOSITE:** Utilitarian slouchy jumpsuits stormed the catwalk in October 1993.

Flashbulbs exploded as Hamnett, dressed in Converse sneakers, white leggings and her own T-shirt emblazoned with the graphic nuclear missile protest '58% DON'T WANT PERSHING' shook hands with the Iron Lady. The stunt escalated the designer's infamy, and the renowned image made headline news on every front page the following day.

Fashion had given Hamnett a voice that she was not afraid to use. Her large block lettering slogan T-shirts popped up everywhere, and were blatantly copied. Slogans included 'SAVE THE SEA', 'EDUCATION NOT MISSILES' and 'CLEAN UP OR DIE'. 'The slogan T-shirt is effective,' she said in 2018, 'Once you've read it, it's in your brain.' Pop stars George Michael and Andrew Ridgeley wore her 'CHOOSE LIFE' T-shirt (a Buddhist mantra) in the video for Wham!'s 'Wake Me Up Before You Go-Go', but her impact on fashion has been far greater than just the powerful slogan T-shirt. Throughout the 1980s and '90s, her brand achieved cult status, reinventing classic workwear pieces that provided a utilitarian aesthetic for both sexes, and in recent years her influence on contemporary menswear has remained a significant force.

With a father in the RAF, Hamnett grew up abroad, living with her family in France and Sweden before being sent to board at Cheltenham Ladies' College in England. After school, she started an advanced diploma in fashion at the highly prestigious St Martin's School

# KATHARINE HAMNETT

# KATHARINE HAMNETT

**OPPOSITE:** Silk bomber jacket worn by presenter and fashion influencer Alexa Chung at London Fashion Week, September 2018

**ABOVE:** All-in-one easy bodysuit made from cotton jersey with *trompe l'oeil print* resembling a jacket, shirt and tie.

of Art in London, where she proved to be an early success, with *Country Life* magazine commenting on her 'interesting outfits' at her graduation show in 1969. At college, she started making her own clothes, and supported herself doing freelance design work. This made her confident enough on leaving college to set up her own company, Tuttabankem, with Anne Buck, an art school friend. The company was successful, selling internationally through Browns in South Molton Street in London and Saks in New York to celebrity clients like Elizabeth Taylor and Marsha Hunt. However, she fell out with her partner, and in 1979, with savings of '500 quid', Hamnett launched her own label.

Determined to be her own boss and always stay independent, the Katharine Hamnett label specialized in stylized appropriation, taking classic military pieces and reinventing them in oversized proportions and interesting fabrics. In 1984, she was named as Designer of the Year by the British Fashion Council and was chosen to kick off the first ever London Fashion Week. To a specially commissioned soundtrack called 'Acid Rain Rap', she showed baggy T-shirts screaming 'WORLDWIDE NUCLEAR BAN NOW', crumpled dark denim unisex trouser suits, oversized parkas with multi-functional pockets, trench coats and padded white silk 'decontamination suits'. The use of brightly coloured parachute silk cut into simple vests and billowing duster coats became a Hamnett staple, and she claims to have invented boiler suits, as well as stonewashed and stretch denim. Reproportioned workwear, duffel coats, sweatshirts, padded silk parkas and bomber jackets that can be worn by both sexes, were early signature pieces that have become much-loved classics she continues to reissue.

At the end of the 1980s, Hamnett discovered the destructive impact the fashion industry was having on the planet and vociferously used her platform to campaign for worldwide change. Becoming a political and environmental activist almost by default, she received very little active support from her own industry and eventually buckled under the uphill struggle of trying to change global manufacturing processes. With her own brand no longer viable, she hooked up with the retailer Tesco in 2007 to sell a sustainable eco collection. In 2014, she relaunched her menswear label, and in 2017 she reopened the Katharine Hamnett London Collection, producing updated archive pieces made only from organic cottons and recycled materials. Her slogan T-shirt was newly updated to reinforce the important message of sustainability: 'BUY NOW WEAR FOREVER'.

# FRANCO MOSCHINO

**ABBIATEGRASSO, ITALY** 1950–1994

**HIGHLIGHTS**
Straitjacket shirt, Magritte-influenced dresses, smiley face logo, rubber ring sculptured hats.

**DESIGN ETHOS**
Irony, humour and surrealism used as visual motifs to poke fun at the industry.

FRANCO MOSCHINO WAS A PROVOCATEUR WHO UTILIZED THE ARTISTIC HUMOUR OF SURREALISM AND DADAISM TO COMMENT ON THE ABSURDITIES OF THE FASHION INDUSTRY AND DISRUPT THE STATUS QUO.

A fashion rebel who throughout his career took aim at the commercial business he was a part of, by using slogans, pronouncements and puns to challenge the vanity and materialism of high fashion. His witty and irreverent messages, such as 'Stop the Fashion System', 'Ready to Where?' and 'This is a Waist of Money' emblazoned directly on the front or back of T-shirts, jackets, dresses and belts became signature tropes, along with his use of surrealist ideas of displacement and visually arresting *trompe l'oeil* imagery. He put paint-like handprints on the shoulder of a beautifully tailored jacket, crafted luxury leather handbags that were decorated with dripping 'melted chocolate' and created a bikini made from watercress that would sprout tiny leaves when watered. He also used recognizable images of doves and blue sky with clouds from the Belgian artist René Magritte and cleverly cut and respliced them together with the nuclear disarmament peace logo and bold typography, for jersey dresses and T-shirts.

Where possible, he upended fashion's norms and expectations; he played with scale, using giant buttons shaped as draughts pieces on a checkerboard dress in 1991, created an inflatable plastic stole that resembled a Lilo to wrap around a crêpe dress in 1996, and sent models down the runway in swaying dresses made up entirely from plastic-coated cards joined to make 'fabric' that were photographically overprinted with imagery of the Taj Mahal in 1997. His imaginative take on fashion was theatrical: catwalk shows were artistic performances, and his shop windows and advertising campaigns were

# FRANCO MOSCHINO

**OPPOSITE:** Franco Moschino with Jeanette Charles appearing as the late Queen Elizabeth II, at the launch party of his new fragrance 'Moschino', 1991.

**ABOVE:** Newsprint fabric was a favourite Moschino trope, from the Spring/Summer Ready-to-Wear collection 1993.

designed to challenge. In 1996, he famously dressed a mannequin in his New York store as Queen Elizabeth II, wearing an elaborate ball gown and a crown constructed entirely from Cheap and Chic cardboard swing tags. The inherent message of mindless consumerism that 'Label Queen' conveyed was shrugged off by Moschino's customers, who loved his sense of humour and unashamedly bought more of his clothes.

At the age of 18, Moschino enrolled at the Accademia di Belle Arti di Brera in Milan to study fine art. After college, he was employed as an illustrator for different magazines before working for a short time as a sketcher for Gianni Versace. For several years he was employed as a designer in the fashion industry in Milan, helping to produce collections for Cadette, Lorenzini, Blumarine and Gianna Cassoli. His first company, Moschino Couture!, was launched in 1983, and press reviews for his inaugural womenswear collection for Summer 1984 labelled him an '*enfant terrible*' and 'bad boy'. Cheap and Chic, a cheaper diffusion line, came in 1988, by which time Moschino's brand of surrealist humour (that often mocked his own customers) was becoming increasingly identifiable through repetitive use of graphic symbols such as a big red heart, a smiley face, a peace logo and a question mark.

Underpinning the visual gimmickry of his collections, the clothes Moschino produced were made from fine-quality fabrics, beautifully cut and finished, and remarkably flattering on the body. Behind the satirical commentary on modern life, Moschino was driven by a moral and social conscience. His was one of the first luxury brands to consider environmental factors with the launch of 'Ecouture' in 1994/95, which used only eco-friendly dyes and materials. He set up charity fashion shows to raise money for the victims of animal abuse, domestic violence and drug addiction and his Smile! Project, launched in 1993, provided support for HIV-positive children in Italy and Romania. In 1994, his ten-year retrospective show, 'X Years of Kaos', showcased some of his most memorable outfits and ended with men, women and children dressed in white and wearing AIDS ribbons. Franco Moschino died shortly after this event at the age of 44, with a charitable foundation set up to continue his philanthropy.

# FRANCO MOSCHINO

**OPPOSITE:** Moschino's pop art, Roy Lichtenstein printed jacket, 1991.

**LEFT:** Humour and irony infiltrated much of Moschino's creative work, and the 'Smiley Face' symbol became a recurring theme in his work, appearing on jackets, bags and key fobs from 1992.

**BELOW:** Multi-coloured, scallop edged jacket with daisy belt and mismatched trousers from the Ready-to-Wear runway show Spring 1993.

# THIERRY MUGLER

**STRASBOURG, FRANCE** 1948–2022

**HIGHLIGHTS**
Metal breastplate designed as a Harley-Davidson motorbike grille, bug eye sunglasses, Botticelli's 'Birth of Venus' dress.

**DESIGN ETHOS**
Exaggerated femme fatale shapes that explore empowerment through dynamic tailoring.

'FASHION IS A GREAT TOOL, BECAUSE IT'S THREE-DIMENSIONAL ART,' THIERRY MUGLER TOLD *WOMEN'S WEAR DAILY (WWD)* IN 2020 ON THE EVE OF HIS MULTIMEDIA RETROSPECTIVE SHOW AT THE MUSÉE DES ARTS DÉCORATIFS IN PARIS.

The designer who dominated the 1980s with his era-defining power suits and theatrical catwalk shows legitimized fantasy in fashion, presenting women as goddesses, superheroes and old-school Hollywood divas.

Taking inspiration from Greek mythology, futurism and nature's creatures (birds, insects, big cats), Mugler was a connoisseur at mixing hard-edged glamour with hyperfeminine sensuality. Rejecting the muted naturalism of loose 1970s hippy styles, Mugler favoured statement tailoring to achieve an exaggerated silhouette. Bold architectural shapes became his signature style, often executed in fabrics not usually associated with couture fashion, such as painted latex, leather, hard-edged plastics, rubber and metal. His spectacular runway shows, choreographed with filmed inserts, thumping soundtracks and celebrity models like Grace Jones, Cyd Charisse and Diana Ross, were made with the production values of a rock concert, entertaining the audience with drama, glamour and elaborate creations. He was often criticized by the press for his misogynistic take on fashion, but Mugler insisted he was always striving for women's emancipation and that many of his original ideas were later considered mainstream.

As a child, Manfred Thierry Mugler had ambitions to be a ballet dancer and from the age of nine he took classes in his home town of Strasbourg, before joining the company of the Opéra National du Rhin at the

## THIERRY MUGLER

**OPPOSITE:** Thierry Mugler takes his applause at the finale of his catwalk show, 1995.

**RIGHT:** Cindy Crawford wears Mugler's iconic Cadillac bustier with handlebars from 1991.

age of 14. The youngest of two sons, with a doctor father and an elegant, creative mother who became Mugler's first muse, his childhood was spent skipping school to visit the local cinema and immerse himself in the glamour of 1930s Hollywood, captivated by the costumes of Edith Head and Travis Banton. By the age of 20 he had moved to Paris, where he initially found employment as a window dresser for a small boutique, and then started selling designs to ready-to-wear fashion companies. He had a spell living in Notting Hill, London, freelancing for Tommy Roberts' Mr Freedom label, before returning to Paris in 1973 to establish Café de Paris, his own first label. Influenced by his training as a ballet dancer, his debut collection of streamlined body-conscious pieces, a trench coat, a little black suit and a 'Siren' dress were in sharp contrast to the folkloric multicoloured ethnic knits that were the hottest trend in Paris. Within two years Mugler founded his namesake company and by the end of the decade he had devised a stylized version of femininity that would become his trademark.

Mugler's extravagant power dressing chimed perfectly with the sensational excess of conspicuous 1980s consumption, and his audacious glorification of 'Superwoman' celebrated a comic book fantasy that emphasized giant shoulders, a push-up bra and a miniscule waist. His view of fashion as being as seductive as a Hollywood movie translated seamlessly to his catwalk presentations, where supermodels shared the adulation with a diverse crowd of older women, drag queens and porn stars.

When MTV exploded on to the small screen, Mugler collaborated with George Michael on his 1992 'Too Funky' video, which featured the hottest supermodels of the day vogueing down the runway in outrageously provocative outfits, creating an iconic fashion/pop moment.

Thierry Mugler stepped down from his own house in 2002, having previously sold out to the French multinational Clarins. The financial success of his two mega-successful fragrances, Angel and Alien, supported his other creative outlets, predominantly photography and costume design. A younger generation of A-list musicians – Lady Gaga, Beyoncé and Cardi B – all endorsed their approval of his *oeuvre*, with specially commissioned outfits for red carpet appearances and stage shows while reality superstar Kim Kardashian wore a body-hugging latex jewelled dress to the Met Gala in 2019. Thierry Mugler died at the age of 73, in 2022.

# THIERRY MUGLER

**OPPOSITE:** Technical theatricality in the form of crinoline-type hooped skirts in acid bright colours.

**LEFT:** The stunning 'Birth of Venus' dress from 1995. It was worn by superstar Cardi B at the 2019 Grammy Awards.

**BELOW:** Claudia Schiffer models a sheer white body-hugging dress, embellished with feathers and silver paillettes, 1995.

# DONNA KARAN

**FOREST HILLS, NEW YORK, USA**
1948–

**HIGHLIGHTS**
'Seven Easy Pieces' mix-and-match stretch separates, wraparound sari skirts, soft blazers.

**DESIGN ETHOS**
Luxury clothes for real women based on comfort and versatility.

REVERED BY THE INDUSTRY AS 'THE QUEEN OF SEVENTH AVENUE', NATIVE NEW YORKER DONNA KARAN CAME TO PROMINENCE IN THE MID-1980S, WHEN SHE CHAMPIONED A MODERN CAPSULE WARDROBE FOR REAL WOMEN OF ALL SHAPES AND SIZES, WHICH REALLY DID WORK FOR EVERYONE.

**BELOW:** Donna Karan on the runway in 1994.

Taking inspiration from her own life, the outspoken designer suggested it was advantageous being a woman, since she could personally relate to the clothes and try things on. 'I want to make life easy; I try to solve problems,' she said.

With her husband Stephan Weiss, Donna Karan launched her namesake business in 1985, focusing on what women needed to keep them looking good throughout a long day. Her 'Seven Easy Pieces' revolutionized clothes for the working woman by simplifying a pared-down set of essentials, centred around a body leotard that could be worn on its own or under other items. This pioneering minimalist wardrobe made in high-quality, soft fabrics consisted of the bodysuit, a tailored jacket, a cashmere sweater, a crisp white shirt, a dress, a skirt and opaque black tights, all of which were designed to be worn in multiple combinations. Karan's updated take on mix-and-match separates that cleverly integrated into numerous outfits that were suitable for the office but could with a few simple accessory tweaks (statement jewellery, high heels) easily transition into late-night chic was a fashion philosophy she went on to develop throughout her career.

Born into the world of fashion in the New York City borough of Queens, Donna Karan's mother was a showroom model and her father a custom tailor.

# DONNA KARAN

**LEFT:** Classic modernity in the shape of perfectly tailored black pants and a crisp white cotton shirt, modelled by Cindy Crawford, 1992.

**BELOW:** A simple sweater dress, belted to emphasize the female form, with matching oversized shearling coat, 1991.

**LEFT:** The diffusion line DKNY appealed to a slightly younger audience with the same aesthetic. Crisp separates of pencil skirt, striped tee and a beret exude a certain French style, from the Ready-to-Wear Collection, 1994.

**OPPOSITE:** A Donna Karan advertisement from 2009, highlights her masterful skill at draping fabric to create fluid, sexy dresses.

'I was practically born with a blazer in my hand,' she has said. She attended Manhattan's prestigious Parsons School of Design for a 'trial' period but quit to get a job as an intern with the sportswear designer Anne Klein, where she started as 'a great pin-picker-upper' before being fired nine months later. Karan then had a brief spell working under Patti Cappalli at Addenda before returning to Anne Klein, where she stayed, working her way up to associate designer in 1971. With the sudden unexpected death of Klein a few years later, a 25-year-old Karan was appointed as chief designer, along with her former Parsons college friend Louis Dell'Olio. Together, they grew the company into a $100 million success story, winning three Coty Awards along the way.

In 1985, Karan launched her own signature line, primarily catering for woman like herself, who led busy lives and were constantly on the go. Women who liked fashion but did not have time to spend hours shopping or putting outfits together embraced her modern, flexible ideas of all-day dressing. She pioneered the use of stretch matte jersey fabric, which supported the body rather than restricting it, creating smart, easy separates, slouchy knitted cardigans, soft leather wrap skirts and cashmere blazers; separates that provided choices for clients who did not have perfect bodies. Her predominantly neutral colour palette with black as a basic staple was offset with occasional contrast brights. The whole concept won immediate acclaim from women who appreciated the ease of her chic city style.

Her diffusion line, DKNY, was launched in 1989. It gained international success, playing on the eclectic buzz of urban city life and aimed at a younger, less affluent audience. In 2015, Karan stepped down as the creative director of her own label, remaining only as an advisor and determined to concentrate on philanthropic projects. Her label Urban Zen launched after she visited Haiti in the aftermath of the 2010 earthquake. It produces seasonless clothes sourced from artisans around the world, her aim being to 'create a culture of community and a more conscious form of consumerism'. Karan is widely regarded as one of the most influential designers of 20th-century womenswear.

# DONNA KARAN

# ISSEY MIYAKE

**HIROSHIMA, JAPAN** 1938–2022

**HIGHLIGHTS**
Bamboo and rattan sculptural bodice, 'Lampshade' dresses, 'Pleats Please', moulded resin bustier.

**DESIGN ETHOS**
New technology and architectural silhouettes fused with traditional Japanese elements of design.

WITH HIS UNIQUE ABILITY TO TRANSFORM THE CONCEPT OF FASHION INTO SOMETHING PROFOUNDLY MORE MEANINGFUL, THE JAPANESE DESIGNER ISSEY MIYAKE PRESENTED HIS FIRST COLLECTION IN PARIS IN 1973 TO IMMEDIATE ADULATION.

BELOW: Issey Miyake, at the Fondation Cartier for contemporary art in 1998.

OPPOSITE: Multi-coloured kaftan dress from the Pleats Please range 1995.

One of a new generation of Eastern designers who challenged the sexualized glamour of modern ready-to-wear clothing, Miyake was revered for his visionary approach, which brought technological fabric innovations to contemporary clothing.

With fashion undergoing a seismic shift towards an emergence of youthful street style, Miyake arrived in the fashion capital with a head full of ideas for future modernity that combined elements of traditional Orientalism with dramatic shapes and silhouettes. Visually, he explored the possibilities of Japanese aesthetics: clothes were magically folded like origami sculptures around the body, uncut and untailored; other pieces resembled protective Samurai body armour. Fabrics were experimental, pushing boundaries of what could be achieved, sometimes gossamer light and ethereal or strangely three-dimensional, moving autonomously around the human form like bouncing lampshades, the results endlessly challenging preconceptions of high fashion. 'I was always interested in making clothing that is worn by people in the real world,' Miyake said in an interview looking back on his career in 2010. Firmly rejecting the title of 'artist', he said, 'I am a designer. I don't make statements. I want to make people happy.'

Miyake's obsessive quest to reject nostalgic dreams in favour of an unwavering curiosity shooting

ISSEY MIYAKE

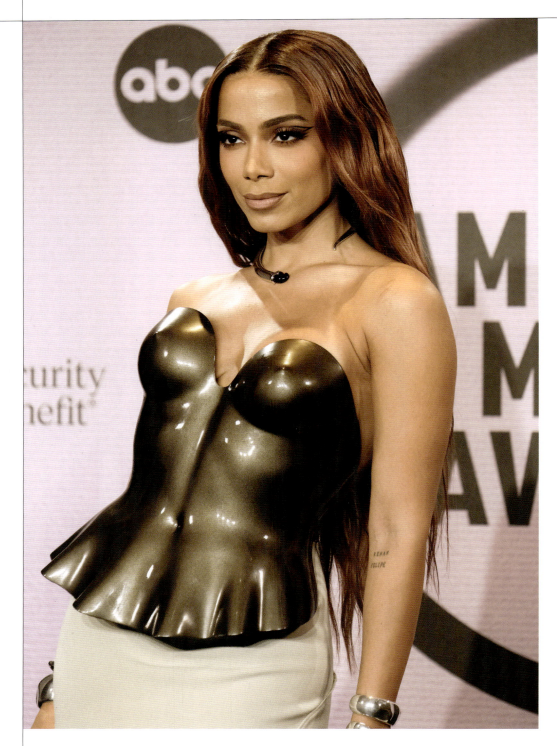

**LEFT:** Bronze coloured, moulded resin bustier, worn on stage by Annita, winner of the 'Favourite Female Latin' award, in Los Angeles, 2022.

**OPPOSITE:** Working with unusual materials Miyake debuted his groundbreaking use of rattan and bamboo, shaped into sunhats and sculptural bodices in 1982.

forwards was directly linked to his own childhood. As a seven-year-old boy he witnessed the catastrophic nightmare of his home town being destroyed by a nuclear bomb. His mother died from radiation poisoning three years later, and Miyake developed osteomyelitis, a bone marrow disease that left him with a permanent limp. Interested in fashion but not sure exactly how to proceed since he had always presumed clothes were a 'European society thing', Miyake instead chose graphic design, and graduated from Tokyo's Tama University in 1964. The following year, with government restrictions relaxed, Japanese people were permitted to travel abroad, and Miyake moved to Paris to study haute couture at the École de la Chambre Syndicale, later finding work as an assistant for Guy Laroche and Hubert de Givenchy. After encountering the violent student protests of May 1968 first-hand, Miyake made a commitment to

# ISSEY MIYAKE

being a part of a new era, and design for a universal public in what he called 'the era of the common man'. A brief stint in New York working for Geoffrey Beene and gaining an understanding of ready-to-wear followed, before he returned to Tokyo in 1970 and set up the Miyake Design Studio. His first collection was shown in New York in 1971 before he presented to an elite Parisian audience two years later.

Unconcerned with trends, Miyake developed an early style of draping, wrapping and layering natural fabrics that became his signature. His ongoing interest in exploring new types of materials (shrunken wools, metallic yarns, straw matting, rattan, bamboo) has intrinsically shaped his direction of design; in the early 1980s he produced moulded resin bustiers that traced the contours of the female body. Beautifully shaped with breasts, torso and navel, flaring out into a peplum frill at the hips, they were produced in a range of vivid colours and designed to be worn like a cuff around the body. In 1993, he launched 'Pleats Please', a revolutionary method of heat-pressing polyester fabric into accordion-like folds that took flight on the body, creating trousers, tube dresses and jackets in amazing shapes that held their line but were easy to wear and care for. The concept of A-POC, 'A Piece Of Cloth', came in 1997, an idea to reduce fabric waste and to involve customer participation, whereby a seamless tube of fabric with outline seams that suggest a dress, shirt, gloves and a hat are individually cut with scissors to create a unique outfit.

Miyake stepped down from day-to-day design duties to concentrate on Reality Lab, a research programme focusing on developing fabrics made from recycled materials, but returned after a 13-year hiatus. The Issey Miyake '132 5.' collection launched in 2010 using computer programming to create three-dimensional outfits from two-dimensional geometric folded fabric patterns; the pursuit to investigate the relationship between clothing and the human form remained paramount.

# VIVIENNE WESTWOOD

**TINTWISTLE, ENGLAND**
1941–2022

**HIGHLIGHTS**
Safety pin Queen Elizabeth II T-shirt, 'Mini-Crini', 'Rocking Horse' shoes, Harris tweed tailoring.

**DESIGN ETHOS**
Celebration of the female form achieved through extensive historical research.

NAMED BY JOHN FAIRCHILD, THE INFLUENTIAL PUBLISHER OF *WWD*, AS ONE OF THE SIX MOST IMPORTANT DESIGNERS OF THE 20TH CENTURY, VIVIENNE WESTWOOD FLAUNTED HER REBEL CREDENTIALS FROM HER 1981 DEBUT SHOW IN LONDON.

Expect the unexpected from an original English eccentric, who first presented a riot of colourful unisex 'Pirates' clothes in the guise of swashbuckling flouncy shirts and printed breeches, and who continually strived to give women their real bodies back in the form of shapely corsets, fitted tailoring and a feminine silhouette.

Dubbed the 'Queen of Punk' for her artfully destroyed, ripped fabrics, other innovations included skinny skirts and dresses made from cotton jersey tubing, and the tie-on bustle. Referencing historical dress, with extensive research from both the 18th and 19th centuries, she established an authentic signature obsessed with traditional shapes and cutting techniques, updating and exaggerating ideas from the past in order to move forwards. Her personal beliefs became public manifestos for her brand, but much in her life was contradictory: though vocally anti-establishment, she famously went to Buckingham Palace to collect her OBE from the Queen, wearing no knickers; and in a bid to help curb climate change and worldwide consumerism, the fashion designer told women to 'stop buying clothes'. Always an outsider – 'the only reason I'm in fashion is to destroy the word "conformity"' she told *The Face* in 1981 – Westwood remained a controversial maverick throughout her long career.

In her late teens, Vivienne Swire dropped out of her silversmithing jewellery course at Harrow School of

# VIVIENNE WESTWOOD

**OPPOSITE:** Dame Vivienne Westwood, 1996 wearing one of her own designs.

**ABOVE:** The infamous 'God Save The Queen' T-shirts sold from Westwood's shop Seditionaries on the Kings Road in 1977.

**RIGHT:** The 'Pirate' collection debuted at Westwood's first ever catwalk show at Olympia London, 1981.

# VIVIENNE WESTWOOD

**OPPOSITE:** Tapping into the heritage of the British Isles, Westwood made Argyll knits, Harris tweed and Scottish tartan significant staples of her career, here shown by Naomi Campbell on the catwalk in 1994.

**RIGHT:** 'Super-elevated Ghillie' platform shoes from the 'Anglomania' collection, 1993.

Art because she didn't think she could possibly earn a living from the art world. She worked as a teacher for several years in a primary school, and met and married her first husband, Derek Westwood. They had a son, but the marriage didn't last long and ended after Vivienne met a brash young art student called Malcolm McLaren. He saw himself as a music Svengali manipulating bands he had put together, such as the Sex Pistols. Together, they opened a small clothes shop at the wrong end of the King's Road with a transient identity that underwent several name changes – Let It Rock, Live Fast Die Young, Seditionaries – as it catered to London's ever-changing youth cults. When the shop reinvented itself as SEX (spelled out in giant pink fluorescent letters above the shop door), Westwood started selling fetishist leather and rubber bondage wear. She printed subversive swastika T-shirts, deconstructing seams and ripping fabric, intuitively homing in on the latest incendiary youth movement that embraced a volatile attitude in both music and fashion.

Their joint contribution to punk catapulted married couple Westwood and McLaren to the epicentre of a new wave of street-inspired British fashion, which kick-started Westwood's ambition to champion the power of women through creativity. After the 'Pirates' collection came another shop, Nostalgia of Mud, and themed collections – 'Savage', 'Buffalo Girls', 'Punkature' and 'Witches' – all of which challenged expectations of fashion, offering asymmetric cuts, unusual fabrics and outsized silhouettes. Westwood and McLaren's personal and professional partnership ended in 1980 but as a part of the Parisian fashion circuit, Westwood had earned critical acclaim on her own.

A change of direction came in 1985 with the introduction of the 'Mini-Crini', the fitted bustier and laced-up 'Rocking Horse' shoes. Fusing two disparate ideas, the Victorian hoop skirt and the modern miniskirt, Westwood's irreverent 'Mini-Crini', printed with outsized polka dots, presented a brand-new silhouette. 'It gives you presence and swings in the most sexy way. Women want to be strong but in a feminine way,' Westwood told *i-D* magazine.

Westwood was one of the first to show underwear as outerwear, placing bras over dresses in the mid-1980s, and established a peculiarly English style as a recognized signature: Miss Marple suits, knitted twinsets and shrunken pony club hacking jackets with giant heart lapels were elevated to high fashion using traditional fabrics like Harris tweeds, tartans and Liberty prints. Inspiration came from sportswear, theatre, rococo fine art from the Wallace Collection, and classical Greece – her vision always imbued with a subversive, often humorous, touch. In 2006, Westwood was awarded the title of Dame Commander of the Order of the British Empire, her originality honoured, but her uncompromising stance to provoke change through fashion remained unabated until her death.

# PAUL SMITH

**NOTTINGHAM, ENGLAND** 1946–

**HIGHLIGHTS**
Photographic prints, contrast print linings, signature stripes.

**DESIGN ETHOS**
Modern tailoring tweaked with an irreverent sense of humour and meticulous attention to details.

'YOU CAN FIND INSPIRATION IN ANYTHING, AND IF YOU CAN'T PLEASE LOOK AGAIN,' IS ENGLISH DESIGNER PAUL SMITH'S MUCH QUOTED ADVICE WHEN TALKING ABOUT HIS DESIGN PROCESS.

With an international reputation for beautifully produced clothes that are classic but never boring, Smith is a genius at quietly evolving his aesthetic, adapting to the changing times and ensuring his worldwide retail empires are packed with sartorial surprises. Having celebrated his 50th year in fashion in 2020, he is credited as being the most successful designer in Britain, revered as a national treasure who has triumphed in a competitive industry without resorting to ostentatious, attention-grabbing gimmicks.

Renowned for his quirky sense of humour that seamlessly translates into his collections, Smith is a keen photographer who captures the minutiae of life wherever he goes; images of flowers, toy robots, food and fluffy white rabbits pop up unexpectedly to add a dash of English eccentricity to his eminently wearable clothes. His multicoloured signature stripe has become the brand's most recognizable pattern, with Smith insisting that each new series of stripes is drawn by hand, not computer generated, to ensure human imperfections. The updated stripes have been

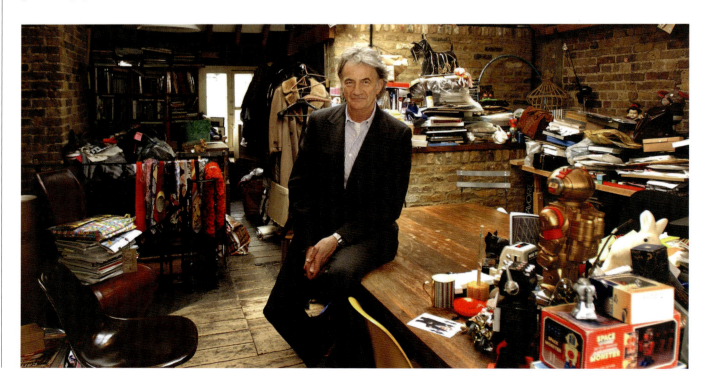

# PAUL SMITH

**OPPOSITE:** Paul Smith in his Covent Garden office, filled with inspirational ephemera, 2003.

**RIGHT:** Decorative flora and fauna prints are regularly re-worked for both men and womenswear collections, shown here in men's suits and matching shirts, 1991.

used subtly inside the collar of a shirt or pocket lining, and rather more blatantly on shirts, dressing gowns, underwear and leather holdalls and have had appeal across a wide spectrum of fans.

Paul Smith grew up in Nottingham and left school at the age of 15, obsessed with cycling and stories of the cool European cycling champions Jacques Anquetil and Fausto Coppi. He rode competitively and had ambitions to compete in the Tour de France, but at 17 he was hit by a car and spent three months in hospital. His enforced stay introduced him to new friends who were part of Nottingham's creative art school crowd; they would go on to influence the direction of his life. With no formal training, he opened his first menswear outlet in Byard Lane, Nottingham, in 1970. It was less of a 'shop' and more of a windowless, damp room that only opened on Fridays and Saturdays, but it had an impressive name – 'Paul Smith, Vêtements Pour Hommes', and sold clothes

(some made by different people) and other collectibles, such as magazines and records.

Smith's retailing skills were honed from this period. 'Since I was 15, I've basically been working in shops, serving people,' he says, always trying to make the customer feel welcome and offering them an interesting mix of merchandise. He whitewashed the walls of a cramped basement in Byard Lane and turned it into a makeshift art gallery, with exhibitions by artists and photographers including David Hockney, Andy Warhol and David Bailey.

Working with his girlfriend (now wife) Pauline Denyer, who had studied fashion at the Royal College of Art in London, Smith grew his business steadily, showing his debut collection in a friend's apartment in Paris in 1976 and opening his first London retail premises in a barely developed Covent Garden in 1979. In the 1980s, Smith reinvented the American boxer brief, taking a boring essential and changing it into a fashionable necessity by adding vibrant colours, playful prints and stripes. He softened the formal suit, making it less corporate and creating a relaxed garment that

## PAUL SMITH

**OPPOSITE:** Stylish casualwear in a soft neutral colour palette offset with black and white stripes from London Fashion Week, 2007.

**ABOVE LEFT:** Model Lily Cole wearing block colour chevron skirt and green satin parka, for Spring/Summer 2008.

**ABOVE RIGHT:** Signature Paul Smith stripes that are re-worked each season, here worn vertically and horizontally in casual menswear from 2024.

allowed men to feel comfortable. Womenswear was introduced in the early 1990s and Smith's pioneering use of realistic photographic images on fabric, creating stunning floral shirts for men and dramatic rose print dresses for women, has become a company staple. A Day-Glo orange plate of waxed spaghetti, intended to be used for restaurant window displays, was found on his travels to Japan, and has since become an iconic Paul Smith signature, emblazoned on T-shirts, swimming trunks, sponge bags and mobile phone cases.

With a healthy distrust of trends and a personal aversion to modern technology (Smith does not do email or allow screens in creative meetings) the company continues to produce classic pieces for people who are confident in the way they look without needing the endorsement of a visible logo, another thing that is anathema to Smith since he feels it plays into people's fashion insecurities. A legion of fans remain loyal to Smith's humorous modernism, including actors John Hamm, Stanley Tucci, Bill Nighy, Vicky McClure and actor/director Greta Gerwig. The company has remained independent, and has more than 160 retail premises in over 60 countries on five continents.

# REI KAWAKUBO

**TOKYO, JAPAN**
1942–

**HIGHLIGHTS**
Asymmetrical black layering, origami cutting, raw edges, shapeless minimalism, goose down padding.

**DESIGN ETHOS**
An artistic approach to the conventions of dress, achieved through brutalist deconstruction.

AS A LEADING FORCE IN A TRIO OF JAPANESE DESIGNERS WHO EXPLODED ON TO THE PARISIAN FASHION SCENE IN 1981, REI KAWAKUBO HAS CONSISTENTLY FLOUTED SOCIETY'S EXPECTATIONS OF BEAUTY, CHALLENGING THE STATUS QUO AND CREATING HER OWN INTELLECTUAL VISION UNINFLUENCED BY LOGIC, SYMMETRY OR PERFECTION.

**BELOW:** Rei Kawakubo at the opening of her Comme des Garçons shop in Henri Bendel's New York, 1983.

Better known by her brand Comme des Garçons ('Like the Boys'), which she founded in 1972, Kawakubo's European debut during Paris fashion week revolutionized the perception of fashion by presenting a collection dominated by shapeless sooty grey and black pieces that defied the superficial norms of glitzy 1980s glamour, best exemplified by the super-bitches of *Dynasty*. Conservative fashionistas in the audience were shocked by the audacity of her unfiltered philosophy; she pioneered the idea that black should be accepted as an everyday fashion staple, and her random, upside-down, inside-out pattern cutting was unlike anything they had previously encountered under the guise of high-end 'fashion'. Dishevelled models with messy hair and flat shoes quietly walked the runway, their bleak, unconventional clothes difficult to comprehend; sisal ropes replaced belts and were slung loosely over shapeless raggedy tunics, fabrics were crumpled and frayed at the edges, jumpers were knitted with deliberate dropped stitches to create

**OPPOSITE:** Deliberately dressing down in the form of distressed, black crumpled dresses, messy hairdos and misplaced lipstick, 1983. New York, 1983.

REI KAWAKUBO

**BELOW:** The 'Lumps and Bumps' collection (1997) on show at New York's Metropolitan Museum of Art Costume Institute, 2017.

**OPPOSITE LEFT:** Defying fashion's sophisticated expectations with a catwalk show championing wild colour, dramatic silhouettes and mis-matched textures and prints, 2018.

**OPPOSITE RIGHT:** Multiple layers of vibrant colour for Spring/Summer Menswear 2019.

ladders and gaping holes. Unnerved by the unorthodox aesthetic Kawakubo presented, the press responded by denigrating her perplexing collection as 'Quasimodo style' and 'apocalyptic end-of-the-world fashion'.

It was clear within a year, however, that her radical reworking of stereotypical femininity was highly influential, with many established designers adopting some of her unfamiliar constructs. Her rejection of mainstream commercial constraints has ensured her progression as a highly successful independent brand.

Rei Kawakubo began her career by completing studies in fine art and literature at Keio University in Tokyo in the early 1960s. Following her graduation, she worked for several years in the advertising department of the Asahi Kasei chemicals and textile company, before becoming a fashion stylist for a short period. With no formal training, she designed her first clothes in 1967, unable to find the sort of things she wanted to wear herself. This inevitably led to her forming her own fashion house, Comme des Garçons, in 1972, and two years later she showed her first collection in Tokyo, opening her first retail outlet in 1976. By 1978, the first menswear collections had been introduced.

Success came alongside that of her Japanese contemporaries, Yohji Yamamoto and Issey Miyake, after exposure at the Paris shows led to international appreciation of new ways of seeing, that celebrated among other ideas, Zen culture. 'I think that pieces that are difficult to wear are very interesting,' Kawakubo

# REI KAWAKUBO

has said. Her favoured methods of deconstruction delight in soft, flowing forms that make a feature of imperfections. She often reconfigures recognizable fashion staples such as men's shirts, re-presenting them weirdly upended, with multiple sleeves latticing across the body like a straightjacket, or cleverly tucked into waistbands, unoccupied arms trailing streamer-like behind.

Her famous 'Lumps and Bumps' collection for Spring/Summer 1997, titled 'Body meets Dress, Dress meets Body', reshaped the female form by introducing amoebic-shaped padding, randomly incorporated into the clothes at the shoulders, neck, back, belly and hips to create unsettling, disfigured body shapes. Constructed from jolly red/white and navy/white stretch Lycra gingham, itself a departure from her usual monochrome palette, Kawakubo commented on the process behind the collection that proposed a new relationship with the way we dress. 'I didn't expect them to be easy garments to be worn every day, but Comme des Garçons clothes should always be new to the world and inspiring.' Fashion journalist Suzy Menkes recalled, 'There was the shock of incomprehension.'

The Comme des Garçons brand has expanded to include diffusion lines and many mainstream collaborations with brands such as Converse. It has also provided a platform that encourages other young designers in the same experimental vein to shine, namely Junya Watanabe and Tao Kurihara. Kawakubo remains one of the most influential designers, whose work often appears in art museums and galleries.

# JEAN PAUL GAULTIER

**ARCUEIL, PARIS, FRANCE** 1952–

**HIGHLIGHTS**
Conical bra corset, men in skirts, *trompe l'oeil* dresses, model diversity.

**DESIGN ETHOS**
Playful provocation, influenced by 1970s punk and 1980s London street style.

PLAYING UP TO HIS MONIKER AS 'THE BAD BOY OF FRENCH FASHION', THE EXUBERANT PERSONALITY OF JEAN PAUL GAULTIER ARRIVED ON THE SCENE IN THE MID-1980S WITH A DADAIST ATTITUDE TO RATTLE THE WELL-MANNERED WARDROBES OF THE PARISIAN BOURGEOISIE.

**BELOW:** Jean Paul Gaultier always recognizable by his matelot T-shirt and peroxide crew cut, 1986.

His catwalk shows challenged the expectations of fashion's purpose to express power and wealth, and he personally wowed the audience with the audacity of his bottle blonde crew cut, kilt and Doc Marten boots. Turning decorum on its head, his signature style embraced all kinds of kitsch, outrageous and demanding ideas: men in skirts, tattooed leggings, *trompe l'oeil* torsos and touches of S&M fetishism.

Sex is his calling card. An obsession with the body and more specifically underwear as outerwear have been recurring themes, with satin corsets and bombshell conical bras his most recognizable tropes. Drawing inspiration from sources as disparate as London's 1980s indie club scene and the opulence of the Folies Bergère, Gaultier upended every expectation about traditional dressing. He was a trailblazer in showing diversity on the catwalk, championing models of every shape, size and ethnicity, and has provoked endless conversation about sexuality, gender and the role of clothes in society.

In 1970, when Jean Paul Gaultier was just 18, he submitted a collection of unedited sketches to the house of Cardin and was offered a part-time job to fit in around his schoolwork. Short periods spent working for other designers – Jacques Esterel, Jean Patou, Angelo Tarlazzi – and working at the style

# JEAN PAUL GAULTIER

**ABOVE LEFT:** Gaultier promoted men in skirts, shown here glittery tartan kilt and leather riding boots, from Autumn/Winter 1999.

**ABOVE RIGHT:** Madonna at the height of her fame, in Gaultier peach satin corset with conical bra; from her Blonde Ambition Tour 1990.

bureau Cincept, and later selling freelance designs to labels like Quorum and Philippe Lelong, shaped his experience in understanding the business of both couture and ready-to-wear. By the age of 25, Gaultier felt experienced enough to launch his own label, but it took several years before he hit his stride. Yet by the early 1980s his shows were receiving rave reviews from the fashion press; *The Face* called him 'the true star of Paris fashion'.

His determination to redefine the parameters of good taste resulted in outrageous avant-garde collections, but underpinning the shock tactics of his shows (boned corset dresses, latex fabrics, gimp

**LEFT:** Clashing tartans became a recurring theme for Gaultier, shown here in an updated frock coat and baggy pants from 1984.

**OPPOSITE:** The concept of underwear as outerwear was promoted, with this boned corset fully exposed under a see-through structured cage dress, 1989.

masks) there was always superb technique, precision tailoring and exquisite craftsmanship. His approach to fashion is unorthodox: 'I love eccentricity, but I am very conservative too,' he told fashion journalist Colin McDowell in 2000, and the ability to fuse a ragtag collection of references, taken from music, movies and street style, jumbled up and then skilfully represented with a humorous twist is his forte.

In 1985, Gaultier presented 'And God created Man' – a collection that shocked the fashion world by introducing male models on his catwalk in skirts. Determined to challenge conventional notions of masculinity, his 'skirts' were actually cut as trousers with a piece of fabric wrapped fluidly over the legs like an apron. His daring approach to menswear has repeatedly suggested an alternative view of gender, showing men in skintight sweaters, buttock-baring trousers, kilts, furs, diamanté and rubber.

His collaboration with Madonna (at the time the most famous woman in the world) for her Blonde Ambition World Tour in 1990 featured his iconic corsetry, which Gaultier claimed was never about sexualizing women but about showing their power. Revealed on stage initially through the strategic slashes of a tailored pinstripe suit, Madonna's pale pink satin corset emphasized a conical spiral-stitched bra, highly structured to exaggerate her body. It became a legendary item of clothing that boosted both their infamy.

Gaultier presented his first haute couture collection in 1997 and was praised for his classical understatement. During a career spanning more than half a century, he has produced perfume ranges, pop records and cinematic costumes. In 2020, Gaultier retired from his own label, which is now overseen by guest designers.

# JEAN PAUL GAULTIER

# CALVIN KLEIN

**NEW YORK, USA**
1942–

**HIGHLIGHTS**
Designer jeans, sporty underwear, provocative advertising campaigns.

**DESIGN ETHOS**
Body-conscious minimalism based on understated sensuality, not practicality.

BUILDING A BRAND THAT WAS BASED ENTIRELY AROUND HIS OWN LIFESTYLE, CALVIN KLEIN CREATED AN EMPIRE THAT SOLD A MODERNIST DREAM OF AMERICA.

**ABOVE:** Calvin Klein in his studio with model Yasmin le Bon, 1985.

Image was everything, and the world bought into his tasteful vision of classic simplicity worn by beautiful people. Before the internet existed, he succeeded in reaching a global audience through a series of ground-breaking advertising campaigns that helped consolidate the company identity, securing his own position as the most famous name in fashion. For a time, he was referred to as America's answer to Yves Saint Laurent, and Klein's sophisticated take on sexy minimalism extended to everything he touched: fashion, make-up, perfume and interiors.

Having seen first-hand in the New York discotheques of the 1970s that jeans could look sensual on women and men, he was the first to introduce the concept of designer jeans. He redesigned the original shape, giving them a button crotch because it was sexier than a zip, making the buttock seam higher and tighter, and embroidering his name on the back pocket. A turning point for his business came with the launch of the now iconic print and TV ads in the early 1980s, featuring a 15-year-old Brook Shields in her figure-hugging jeans.

'You want to know what comes between me and my Calvins? Nothing.' the voiceover purred. Moral outrage erupted and sales immediately skyrocketed to 200,000 pairs a week.

Klein grew up in a middle-class area of the Bronx and was encouraged by both his father (an immigrant from Hungary who ran a greengrocer's shop) and his artistic mother to pursue his interests in fashion, art and design. He studied fashion at New York's Fashion Institute of Technology (FIT)

# CALVIN KLEIN

**LEFT:** Klein's underwear sales skyrocketed after the success of his huge Times Square billboard campaigns. American athlete Tom Hintinhous stopped traffic in his white cotton briefs, 1982.

**BELOW:** The teenage Brooke Shields' infamous strap line 'Nothing comes between me and my Calvins' became one the most memorable advertising slogans ever in the 1980s.

but left before he graduated, finding employment with a series of garment manufacturers on Seventh Avenue, including Dan Millstein. With an initial loan of $10,000 from his childhood friend Barry Schwartz (who became his lifelong business partner), Klein set up their company in 1968 to produce contemporary coats and suits. Targeting a young audience who would not contemplate buying expensive clothes,

# CALVIN KLEIN

**OPPOSITE:** Cindy Crawford in neutral shades and luxury fabrics, which defined Klein's sophisticated contribution to fashion in the early 1990s.

**RIGHT:** Silver lace evening gown with fitted bra top and shoestring straps, worn by Karen Mulder for Spring 1992 Ready to Wear collection.

Klein said he 'saw a void in the market. The level beneath couture interested me, clothes that are good-looking but also young.' Stylish separates designed to be multifunctional and made from good-quality fabrics – cashmere, suede, linen and fine wools – in a neutral colour palette became his signature, all aimed at a burgeoning demographic of young professionals.

At the start of his career, Klein was mentored by Baron Nicolas de Gunzburg, a powerful arbiter of taste who worked as a senior fashion editor at American *Vogue*. Gunzburg was instrumental in encouraging the designer's aesthetic development and introducing him to New York's elite society figures. In September 1969, a winter coat of his appeared on the cover of *Vogue*, a strong endorsement of his emerging talent as a young designer and also recognition of America's growing status within the fashion industry.

With a growing emphasis on marketing sex and sensuality, promoting Klein's increasing range of products became his forte, the visual identity of the brand so much aligned with the man himself. Relying heavily on input from a crew of talented collaborators, Klein set up his own in-house advertising company to sell his products. The homoerotic imagery created by Bruce Weber for Klein's designer underwear caused controversy, as did pictures of a near-naked Kate Moss for the perfume Obsession. Klein was the first to introduce a unisex fragrance, CK One, in 1994, promoted with Steven Meisel's black-and-white images of a gang of grungy rebellious kids who looked a world away from high fashion and captured the anti-glamour zeitgeist of the times. 'I was always trying to appeal to a wide range of people: gay, straight, young, old,' he told Marc Jacobs in 2013.

Klein stepped down from his own company in 2002, having achieved his ambition to build a brand that continues to exist long after his departure.

# GIORGIO ARMANI

| **PIACENZA, ITALY** 1934 |
|---|
| **HIGHLIGHTS** Deconstructed suits made from crumpled fabrics, Richard Gere's wardrobe in *American Gigolo*, greige (beige plus grey). |
| **DESIGN ETHOS** Restrained sophistication and 'less is more' elegance, based on the eternal values of timeless luxury, not transient trends. |

'I DETEST FASHION WHEN IT BECOMES GROTESQUE,' GIORGIO ARMANI TOLD A FASHION JOURNALIST IN THE EARLY 1990S, HAVING BUILT A GLOBAL REPUTATION FOR MAKING MEN LOOK SEXY IN SOFT UNSTRUCTURED SUITS.

His entrance into a mass-market audience came via Richard Gere's effortlessly cool wardrobe in the 1980 film *American Gigolo*, which catapulted the relatively unknown designer to worldwide fame. His radical approach to menswear (and later womenswear) revolutionized the traditional dynamics of tailoring; he abolished the rigid formality of suiting by removing internal padding and linings, softened the shoulder line and instead presented a looser cut, using lightweight fabrics in modern colours. This aesthetic, which cultivated comfortable power dressing for both sexes, dominated the 1980s and the Armani name became a byword for sophisticated Italian style.

With impeccable timing, his deconstruction of old-style trouser suits provided a contemporary new uniform for a liberated generation of working women making strides in the boardroom. As a visible figurehead, Armani's quest for perfection is legendary; his label guaranteed clients luxury in an understated style without resorting to ostentatious gimmickry. 'I admire discretion and I loathe exhibitionism,' he says. His ethos to evolve slowly and create 'must-have' products with longevity that reflect the core values of his company resulted in numerous lines of diversification. In 1991, he launched Armani Exchange in America, a mass-market affordable range that

**ABOVE:** Giorgio Armani celebrating another successful catwalk show in Milan.

# GIORGIO ARMANI

caters for a younger audience, but Emporio Armani, Armani Jeans, Armani/Casa homewares, Armani Junior and a collection of profitable fragrances have all contributed to the success of the Armani fashion empire for more than 40 years.

With a childhood that was deeply affected by World War II, and living in a part of Italy that was under constant bombardment, Giorgio Armani's close relationship to his Italian family has consistently influenced his work ethic and sense of motivation. His distinguished father, Ugo Armani, worked as a shipping manager and his 'exceptionally elegant' mother, Maria, taught him the fundamental principles of dignity and self-respect, both subsequently adopted in his life and career.

With early ambitions to be a doctor, Armani studied for two years at the University of Piacenza before realizing it was not the right path for him. An interest in the Hollywood movies of the 1950s (Cary Grant was his favourite leading man) and a wider fascination for the creative arts led him to Milan, where he worked initially as a window dresser, and later as a manager and then a buyer at the department store La Rinascente, where he learned a great deal about fashion. Without formal training, he found employment as an apprentice with Nino Cerruti,

**ABOVE LEFT:** Fluid tailoring and a soft colour palette offset by crisp white piping details from the Spring Ready-to-Wear collection in 1987.

**OPPOSITE:** Couture craftsmanship showcased in the Autumn/Winter 2014 collection.

**BELOW LEFT:** Actor Richard Gere in *American Gigolo* with wardrobe by Armani. The 1980 film swiftly catapulted Armani's reputation to a global audience.

a prestigious menswear company, where he was encouraged to find ways to make a suit less industrial and more comfortable.

Armani set up his own business in 1975, opening his first retail store in Milan with his business partner Sergio Galeotti, both determined to explore new concepts in men's fashion, to create clothes that facilitated ease of movement, and to investigate ideas of a softer masculinity. At the age of 40, Armani designed with himself in mind, disregarding the cardboard suits his own father had worn; instead, he invented a new silhouette, modifying proportions, changing the alignment of the buttons, choosing neutral-coloured linens and creating something relevant for his own generation.

With the phenomenal impact of Armani's stylish wardrobe for Hollywood heart-throb Richard Gere in 1980, in what became a celebrated movie, international success came quickly. Responding to requests from his sister Rosanna, and applying the same basic principles, Armani expanded into womenswear, launching collections that offered powerful femininity without compromising on comfort.

Loyal fans claim his perfect pieces never date, and he has long been a promoter of sustainable fashion, endorsing the production of high-quality garments that are never influenced by trends and are designed to last. With no obvious successor to take over, there has been much talk about the long-term future of the privately owned company, which had an annual revenue of 2.35 billion euros in 2022. Armani himself remains the sole shareholder of a business he set up in the 1970s, and is personally responsible for all creative and business decisions.

GIORGIO ARMANI

# CHRISTIAN LACROIX

| **ARLES, SOUTH OF FRANCE** 1951– |
|---|
| **HIGHLIGHTS** <br> 'Pouf' and bustle, embossed fabrics, religious iconography, decorative cropped jackets. |
| **DESIGN ETHOS** <br> Extreme sensory overload achieved through masterful juxtaposition of colour, print and texture. |

**BELOW:** Christian Lacroix prepares for a show in his Parisian studio, 1987.

IRREPRESSIBLY EXUBERANT AND INSTANTLY RECOGNIZABLE BY THE GRAND HAUTE COUTURE SIGNATURES EMBODIED IN HIS WORK, CHRISTIAN LACROIX SHOOK UP EXPECTATIONS OF FASHION IN THE 1990S, BECOMING A MAJOR FORCE OF THE DECADE.

Visually stunning collections celebrated extravagant excess, through his unique adoption of contrasting prints, clashing vibrancy and dramatic silhouettes. Models sashayed playfully down the runway in a riot of opulence that successfully collaged contrasting styles and historical references. His celebrated shortie 'Pouf' bubble skirt, an updated interpretation of a 19th-century crinoline contrasted with his *toreador*-style capes. Ruffles, flounces and oversized bows, traditional elements of couture, took on a modern iconography in the lurid colours of his Mediterranean home town. With a magician's touch, rosebud florals swirled alongside spots and stripes and heavy brocades were offset by delicate lace, endorsing

# CHRISTIAN LACROIX

**RIGHT:** Lacroix at his best, successfully mixing colour, texture and silhouette to create his dramatic vision, 1991.

**LEFT:** Taking cues from historical dress with embellishment firmly focused at the back of this orange satin evening gown, 1998.

**OPPOSITE:** Multiple prints, colours and beaded decoration take centre stage at the Autumn 1999 Couture show.

a 'more is more' aesthetic with many items heavily embellished with beading and embroidery to showcase the intricate expertise of hand-finishing associated with high-level luxury.

Lacroix's enthusiasm for exaggerated fashion statements took references from multiple sources: art, theatre, street style, the flea market, historical costume and his Provencal childhood. His genius lay in the juxtaposition of disparate elements, which skilfully mixed historical chronology and geographical heritage. Every season, Lacroix revealed myriad new ideas, shapes and silhouettes, resulting in brilliantly uplifting collections that provoked unanimous admiration from an international audience bored of the ubiquitous boxy power suit.

Born in the Provençal city of Arles, Christian Lacroix grew up sketching historical costumes and fashion. He has recounted an early family anecdote from the 1950s of his grandfather enquiring of all his young grandchildren, 'What do you want to be when you grow up?' Lacroix apparently shouted out, 'Christian Dior'. After school, he studied history of art and museum studies at the Sorbonne and École du Louvre in Paris with a view to being a curator. His transition to fashion started with work as an assistant at Hermès, and then at Guy Paulin, where he specialized in accessories.

In 1981, he was given the remit to revitalize the house of Patou, specifically to increase clothing sales for a couture house whose reputation was significantly dependent only on perfume sales. The

# CHRISTIAN LACROIX

ambition was always to create something more operatic and baroque – Lacroix wanted to rediscover 'the exuberance of haute couture' and find a new direction for the 1980s. His time at Patou allowed him to develop his own style, culminating in a showstopping collection in 1986 that featured short bubble dresses and contemporary-style bustles on strapless evening gowns.

By 1987, with the financial backing of Dior's parent company Financière Agache, Lacroix was eager to launch his own couture house, with a ready-to-wear line and the opportunity for lucrative licensing deals to follow. His debut collection in October 1987 sent ecstatic shock waves through the whole of Paris, undeniably significant since it was the first couture house to open since 1962; the press hailed his eclectic theatricality a sensation and declared him the long-awaited successor to Yves Saint Laurent. His voluminous bubble skirt, cut short and often tucked up at the back, became the most successful aesthetic of late 1980s party wear, copied by other designers and reproduced in cheap fabrics for mass-market consumption on the high street. Lacroix's ornate couture dresses, which were crazily expensive, and often wildly over-the-top, were always a big hit with A-list celebrities and red-carpet film stars who craved both glamour and attention.

The recession of the 1990s dented Lacroix's meteoric trajectory as fashion adopted a more sober tone, and Bazaar, his diffusion line, provided a cheaper alternative to reflect the changing economic times. The company closed the couture and ready-to-wear business in 2009, but the name has continued with accessories, homeware and perfumes. In 2013, Lacroix designed a one-off haute couture collection of 18 pieces for the House of Schiaparelli. His flamboyant use of colour and emphatic signature of oversized bows aligned his creativity with that of the surrealist designer who loved to shock her customers. Lacroix's modern interpretation of Schiaparelli's *oeuvre*, which included giant candy stripes, pom-pom-adorned Pierrot hats and oversized pocket details, ignited interest in the relaunch of the dormant label. Lacroix's dazzling contribution as one of fashion's most imaginative exponents remains undiminished.

# MARTIN MARGIELA

## GENK, BELGIUM

1957–

### HIGHLIGHTS
XXL oversized, one-armed silhouette, inside-out seams, sweater made from socks, tabi shoes.

### DESIGN ETHOS
Deconstructionism that challenges traditional concepts of high-end fashion.

**BELOW:** The elusive Belgian designer, Martin Margiela.

THE CONCEPTUAL, EXPERIMENTAL COLLECTIONS OF THE RECLUSIVE OUTSIDER MARTIN MARGIELA TURNED HIM INTO A CULT DESIGNER, REVERED BY FASHION 'INSIDERS' WHO APPRECIATED HIS MASTERFUL REINTERPRETATION OF CLOTHES, AND INTELLECTUAL EXAMINATION OF LUXURY.

He presented ballet shoes as evening bags, T-shirts constructed out of plastic bags, and used hessian and toile muslin for jackets. Known as the most radical of the Antwerp designers, he came to prominence in 1989, when his ideas challenged stereotypical norms of dress and upended traditional ways of presenting fashion. Margiela, who refused to

be photographed or conduct face-to-face interviews with journalists, set his own unconventional agenda, and early improvisations and creative solutions for MMM (Maison Martin Margiela) established a 1990s anti-fashion aesthetic that became increasingly influential to the mainstream. Diametrically opposed to the flash, slick, power dressing of the previous decade, Margiela's vision was to develop offbeat ideas of deconstructionism, presenting clothes in a revisionist way that appeared strangely beautiful; seams were left exposed, pockets were inverted, hems were unfinished, half-constructed linings were visible and tailored pieces were worn inside out and upside down. His rejection of corporate branding inspired an immaculate white fabric label held in place by four perfect stiches, the omission of his name on these 'ghost labels' only adding to the mystique of this anonymous, enigmatic designer and contributing to his success.

Graduating in 1979 from the Royal Academy of Fine Arts in Antwerp, Margiela became known as the most revolutionary of the Belgian avant-garde designers. He was associated, but not directly involved with,

**OPPOSITE:** Deconstructed denim dress, made from multiple pieces of workwear, 1999

MARTIN MARGIELA

**LEFT:** Decorative *trompe l'oeil* lingerie slip, printed onto the back of a fluid shift dress from 1999.

**OPPOSITE:** Confounding expectations of fashion Margiela presents his raw edged leather jacket made up entirely of disparate leather belts, 2006.

# MARTIN MARGIELA

the Antwerp Six, an influential fashion collective that included Dries Van Noten, Dirk Bikkembergs and Ann Demeulemeester. Having met his future business partner Jenny Meirens at a prestigious textile industry award, the Golden Spindle, in 1983, he agreed to sell his competition collection through her independent shop, Crea, a multi-brand boutique she owned.

Gaining hands-on experience as a freelance designer for five years, including a few years in the mid-1980s working as an assistant to Jean Paul Gaultier, Margiela was ready to launch his own label by 1988. With Meirens alongside him, many of the early creative decisions that were taken were born out of necessity due to lack of finances. Without the cash to fund a central venue for his shows, he made models walk in wastelands, and decrepit warehouses on the outskirts of Paris; invitations were published in free newspapers; and the audience would have to stand and watch. He painted walls, floors and ceilings of an empty hangar white and lit the space with candles, showed his collections in a cemetery at Montmartre, and in a circus tent at the Bois de Boulogne, his alternative presentations becoming as much a recognized signature of Margiela's unconventional style as his constant dissection and reconstruction techniques.

Extreme proportions, exaggerated silhouettes and surrealist devices of *trompe l'oeil* (jackets made from tailors' 'paper pattern' pieces) have all been explored as recurring themes in his collections, and much of Margiela's innovative output comes from reimagining and recycling objects as well as clothing. Broken plates held with wire become a waistcoat, army socks are refashioned into a jumper, forks are turned into bracelets and often incongruous garments are pulled apart and simply added to an existing outfit to create an unfamiliar example of displacement theory with raw edges, visible stitches and shoulder padding deliberately exposed.

In 1997, the media-shy designer, who only ever responded to interview questions by fax, was hired by Jean-Louis Dumas as creative director of women's ready-to-wear at the luxury label Hermès. Claiming he wanted the clothes to do the talking, and not his persona, he told *WWD* (by fax) that his

debut collection would continue 'a sensitivity to the transcendence of quality, tradition, craftsmanship and comfort'. Margiela's appointment was intriguing to some fashion journalists, but his cult following provided a new fashion audience eager to witness his love of tailoring exemplified through the collections of a superluxe heritage brand.

In 2000, Margiela provided a commercial collection for the 3 Suisses catalogue, alongside Karl Lagerfeld, Thierry Mugler and Jean Paul Gaultier. Widely acknowledged as a fashion disrupter who has consistently redefined fashion's tasteful boundaries, Margiela retired in 2009 to pursue a career as an artist. Subsequent collections were designed by his atelier team and in 2015 John Galliano was appointed creative director.

# AZZEDINE ALAÏA

**TUNIS, TUNISIA**
1935–2017

**HIGHLIGHTS**
Knitted bandage dresses, studded eyelet rings in leather, laser-cut lace patterns.

**DESIGN ETHOS**
Timeless clothes that celebrate the female figure, redundant of fashion trends or gimmicks.

THE DIMINUTIVE FRANCO-TUNISIAN AZZEDINE ALAÏA WAS REVERED WITHIN THE FASHION WORLD AS THE 'KING OF CLING', KNOWN AS A TRUE INNOVATOR WHO ADORED WOMEN AND SIMPLY WANTED EVERYONE HE DRESSED TO LOOK SEXY AND BEAUTIFUL.

**BELOW:** Azzedine Alaïa in the shadow of model Beverley Peele, in New York 1994.

'My obsession is to make women wonderful,' he said. 'When you create with that in mind things can't go out of fashion.' His meticulous craftsmanship created womenswear that blurred the lines between fashion and art with perfection achieved through great technical ability to sculpt 'second skin' fabric around the female form. With his workaholic mentality, which valued creativity over commerce, Alaïa cared passionately about the flawless execution of a garment, often ironing things himself to ensure the finish he required. Wealth and personal fame were of little interest to him; a fashion maverick unprepared to sacrifice the quality of his craft to adhere to the seasonal demands of the Fashion Week schedules, he only showed his collections at a time and place when he considered them ready.

His clientele was stellar, with the world's biggest celebrities clamouring to be dressed by him – Madonna, Grace Jones, Tina Turner and Paloma Picasso were all vocal fans, as were the original 1990s supermodels (Linda Evangelista, Naomi Campbell, Tatjana Patitz, Cindy Crawford), who would do whatever they could to change dates in order to

**RIGHT:** Singer and actor Grace Jones storms the runway in classic 'second skin' Alaia from 1986.

# AZZEDINE ALAÏA

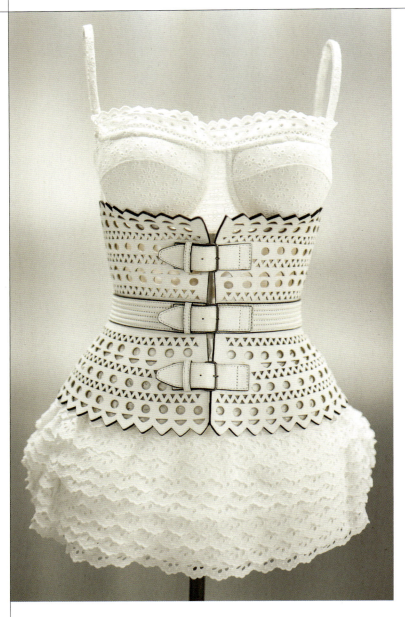

appear in his show. Alaïa established a modern body-conscious aesthetic that changed little over a 30-year career. Sculptural corsets, flared skirts of varying lengths and high-heeled ankle boots were staples that celebrated women's femininity, all undatable pieces that became elegant classics, never influenced by the vagaries of 'fashion'.

Born in the town of Tunis at the far north-eastern tip of Africa, Alaïa was influenced at an early age by the women in his family: a twin sister, Hafida, his mother, aunts,

And grandmother and the family midwife who worked as a dressmaker and introduced him to Parisian fashion magazines. He briefly studied sculpture at the Institut Supérieur des Beaux-Arts in Tunis, before leaving for a promised job at Christian Dior in Paris in 1957. Without the appropriate paperwork, the position lasted only five days, but he found work creating costumes for the cabaret dancers at the Crazy Horse as well as periods with Guy Laroche and Thierry Mugler.

Throughout the 1970s demand grew for Alaïa's couture skills, and he consolidated his reputation with exquisite gowns for a niche group of aristocrats and actresses, including the novelist Louise de Vilmorin, Cécile de Rothschild, Greta Garbo and Marlene Dietrich. In 1980, he presented his first ready-to-wear collection of figure-hugging leather pieces, which set a precedent for what was to come. His manipulation of a material not previously associated with fluidity became legendary. In his hands, leather became as supple as silk, creating flouncy skirts, fitted bra tops and voluminous trench coats. Unlike most couturiers, who embellish with decorative surface detailing, Alaïa used technology to incorporate pattern within the material: stamping metal eyelets and studs into fabric, creating open seams with fretwork stitches and laser-cutting complex 'lace' patterns on to hemlines and footwear.

His explorations from 1986 onwards with elastic knit fabrics that wrapped around the body to create 'bandage dresses' became a revolutionary moment in fashion history, ushering in a decade of bodycon dressing that defined the 1990s. Black was a favourite colour, but also a softer palette that reflected the shifting shades of the Sahara Desert, such as olive, khaki, brown and variations of nude; in Alaïa's skillful hands even head-to toe-leopard skin Lycra could become an empowering fashion statement.

Alaïa withdrew from the fashion circuit in the early 1990s after the death of his twin sister, although he continued to produce an occasional limited-edition collection and still undertook exquisite couture commissions for private clients. He sold his company to Prada in 2000, buying it back again in 2007, and later selling a stake to the luxury group Richemont.

# AZZEDINE ALAÏA

**OPPOSITE:** Laser cut corset belts became a signature part of Alaïa's collections from the 1990s onwards.

**RIGHT:** Body conscious cutting with precision lacing over the torso from spring 2003.

# JIL SANDER

| **WESSELBUREN, GERMANY** 1943– |
|---|
| **HIGHLIGHTS** Tailored trouser suit, white T-shirt, unstructured trench coat. |
| **DESIGN ETHOS** Modernity without banality, 'Future forward without being futuristic'. |

AT A TIME WHEN GERMAN DESIGNERS WERE ALMOST INVISIBLE ON THE INTERNATIONAL FASHION CIRCUIT, JIL SANDER ARRIVED WITH HER BRAND OF UNDERSTATED MINIMALISM THAT MADE THE GLITZY EXCESSES OF THE 1980S LOOK THEATRICALLY VULGAR.

**BELOW:** Jil Sander in Milan 2004.

Uncompromising in her vision, Sander rejected the ostentatious stereotype of femininity, offering instead impeccable ideas that promised a perfectly pared-down wardrobe. 'Everything needed to be done differently,' she said of her philosophy, providing women with the essential pieces that offered uncomplicated choices and boosted confidence.

Her streamlined collections, executed with architectural precision in luxurious fabrics, were effortlessly elegant but never dull. Known in the fashion world as the 'Queen of Minimalism', signature staples included a button-down cotton shirt, navy cashmere trench coat, a perfect white T-shirt and classic suit pants, which offered the comfort of longevity to women who shunned fleeting commercial trends or statement dressing, to boost their self-worth. Sander herself epitomized the brand, a confident figurehead of modernity who exploited the attitude of intelligent minimalism to win respect. It was her discerning eye, honed as a fashion editor and constantly questioning the purity of line, proportion and silhouette of the clothes she was using in her editorial stories, that led to her creating her own collections. 'Pureness' is not as easy as it looks, she says, explaining the ethos that underpinned her success. 'Even if things end up looking easy, we know how difficult it is to make things appear effortless.'

Brought up in the northern German port of Hamburg, Sander credits the brilliance of light in her

# JIL SANDER

home town location for igniting a passion for colour and textural tone in the materials she later sought out. Early studies included textile design and textile engineering, but at the age of 18 Sander went to the University of California, Los Angeles for two years on a foreign exchange programme, where the laid-back lifestyle, hospitable climate and relaxed attitudes to casual sporty dress codes shaped her future direction.

**ABOVE:** Classic layered tailoring, in the form of sharp belted trouser suits worn under easy, unstructured coats from the Autumn Ready-to-Wear collection from 1991.

**LEFT:** Making a statement through tonal use of a single colour, in a fitted suit with pencil skirt worn under a roomy wool duster coat, 1992

**OPPOSITE:** Cream wool pea coat worn over matching pants, and bright red shift dress shaped by clever cutting of circular seams, from the Autumn/Winter collection 2004.

Starting work in the mid-1960s as a fashion editor on German magazines *Constanze* and *Petra*, Sander was constantly dissatisfied with the clothes she was using to shoot fashion stories, critical of both the fit and the fabrics that were used at the time. Approaching the manufacturers to helpfully suggest useful alterations, she began freelance designing, thinking she could do a better job.

Sander opened her first boutique in Hamburg in 1968, selling clothes she had handpicked from a couple of French and Italian designers and some of her own one-off designs. The brand evolved slowly, the intention from the early 1970s to reappropriate the modern principles of the male wardrobe and apply them to women, totally eliminating unnecessary decoration. She showed her collection in Paris for the first time in 1975, extolling the virtues of minimalism alongside a wave of new Japanese designers who offered a similar aesthetic, but it took a while for her radical modernism to make its mark.

Sander's trademark classics are defined by the idea that luxury comes from the impeccable quality of the fabric; she prefers to use traditional menswear fabrics in subdued, sophisticated colours that allow the individual personality, rather than the outfit, to make an impact. By the 1990s, Sander had established international success with her beautifully tailored essentials that worked for women, helped in part by a series of critically acclaimed advertising campaigns that featured the elite supermodels Linda Evangelista and Shalom Harlow. In 1999, Sander sold 75 per cent of her company to the Italian company Prada and has since returned and then resigned again from the brand that still bears her name. In 2009 and 2020, she teamed up with Japanese-founded Uniqlo to produce popular capsule collections for a mass market that retail under the +J label.

JIL SANDER

# GIANNI VERSACE

**CALABRIA, ITALY**
1946–1997

**HIGHLIGHTS**
Punk safety pin dress worn by Liz Hurley at the premiere of *Four Weddings and a Funeral*, fluid chain mail evening dresses, Marilyn Monroe/James Dean print dress.

**DESIGN ETHOS**
Glitz and glamour, dazzling colour and embellishment combined with classical Greek imagery.

IF THE ACCEPTABLE FACE OF ITALIAN FASHION IN THE 1980S WAS SOFT TAILORING IN THE FORM OF NEUTRAL-COLOURED LINENS, THEN THE GLITZY SEX-BOMB AESTHETIC THAT GIANNI VERSACE CHAMPIONED TOWARDS THE END OF THE DECADE DRAMATICALLY CHANGED THAT NARRATIVE.

**BELOW:** Siblings, Gianni Versace with his younger sister Donatella in the early 1990s.

His colour-infused catwalk presentations screamed *la dolce vita*; printed fabrics luxuriously embellished with sequins and beading evoked provocative Italian glamour, creating a visual impact that was irresistible when channelled through the exuberant swagger of the 'Glamazon' supermodels. Versace was the first to unite the 'Supers' on the catwalk, having already used them in his advertising campaigns, and when Cindy, Linda, Naomi and Christy stormed on to the runway to close his 1991 show, holding hands and lip-syncing to George Michael's 'Freedom! '90' (the singer was watching from the front row), fashion changed forever. 'He made fashion a pop culture phenomenon,' Claudia Schiffer said recently.

Versace capitalized on sexuality and celebrity, dressing famous friends like Elton John for his world tour and album covers, adept at utilizing an allegiance between fashion and music to boost publicity. His catwalk presentations were staged as contemporary rock shows with theatrical lighting effects and staged choreography, played out before an audience of A-list stars like Madonna, Tupac Shakur and Prince. Consolidating his signature tropes of bold prints that merged classic and modern imagery, his colour palette relied on intense brights juxtaposed with black and gold. His flamboyant personality pushed boundaries,

# GIANNI VERSACE

**LEFT:** Clashing prints inspired by flamboyant Rococo style ornamentation with additional embellishment typified much of Versace's output in the early 1990s.

**ABOVE:** A then-unknown Elizabeth Hurley attending the premiere of her boyfriend Hugh Grant's film *Four Weddings and a Funeral* in London in 1994. Versace's safety pin dress made her an overnight sensation and also boosted his reputation as the king of red-carpet dressing.

exploiting ideas of S&M into decorative high fashion, realized in supple black leather, with studs, straps, buckles and everywhere the golden Medusa head that represented Versace.

The brand quickly established a strong identity, producing collections that were immediately recognizable. When Elizabeth Hurley stepped out to the premiere of *Four Weddings and a Funeral* in 1994 in a dress constructed entirely of strategically cut strips of fabric held together with elaborate oversized gold safety pins, the paparazzi went crazy, and the name Versace subsequently appeared on every international newsstand.

Surrounded by the sparkling waters of the Ionian Sea at the southernmost tip of Italy, the elegant town of Reggio Calabria was home to Gianni Versace,

# GIANNI VERSACE

**OPPOSITE:** Tapping into the immediacy of pop culture as a source of inspiration Versace created prints with multi-coloured images of James Dean and Marilyn Monroe, as well as parodying his own industry with images of *Vogue* magazine. Mannequins on display at the Fashion Institute of the Metropolitan Museum of Art, in New York, 1997.

**BELOW:** Helena Christensen stalks the Paris runway, in zebra print coat and leopard print leggings, from the Spring/Summer Haute Couture collection 1996.

who grew up watching his dressmaker mother stitch bridal gowns for local women. He later worked for his mother's business before moving north to Milan in the early 1970s, where he started designing suede and leather collections for Genny, Callaghan and Complice. After five years as a successful freelance designer, he was ready to set up his own business with his elder brother Santo and sister Donatella, who were an integral part of the family company.

His first collection shown under the Gianni Versace label was launched in 1978 at the Palazzo della Permanente in Milan. Early collections excelled in wearable daywear in muted, earthy colours, and he experimented with methods of classical draping, taking inspiration for wrapping lengths of fabric around the body from traditional Indian and Turkish costume. From 1983 onwards he was regularly commissioned to design theatre, opera and ballet costumes for the grandest productions in Europe, from La Scala in Milan to Covent Garden in London, and the theatricality of his costumes clearly crossed over into the showmanship of his fashion collections. Memorable designs successfully combined Warhol's pop art imagery into iconic fashion pieces, and multicoloured faces of Marilyn Monroe were printed on to silk leggings and body-hugging evening gowns, adorned with rhinestone gems and glass beads. He also invented oroton, a unique chain mail-type metal mesh in gold or silver that fell as fluidly as silk when cut into column dresses reminiscent of Greek goddesses, which became a house staple.

In 1997, at the height of his fame, Versace was tragically murdered outside his home in Miami. His sister Donatella Versace has continued to head up the company.

# KARL LAGERFELD

**HAMBURG, GERMANY**
1933–2019

**HIGHLIGHTS**
Updated invention of the original LBD, blockbuster catwalk shows for Chanel, branded CC motorbike boots.

**DESIGN ETHOS**
Street style and contemporary culture subverted with irreverence to create luxury high fashion.

DURING THE 20TH CENTURY, THE STATUS OF FASHION DESIGNER MORPHED INTO THE REALM OF CELEBRITY CULTURE, AND NOBODY EXEMPLIFIED THIS BETTER THAN KARL LAGERFELD, WHO WAS OFTEN REFERRED TO AS 'KING KARL'.

With a mega-successful career that was prolific in scope, spanning over five decades, Lagerfeld was the ultimate fashion chameleon. His workaholic mentality generated simultaneous collections for a handful of luxury brands and his refusal to confine himself to working exclusively for just one company elevated his prominence as a freelance creative director. With an unsurpassed knowledge of fashion history drawn from an encyclopaedic love of reading, his ability to exploit the zeitgeist of an era proved infallible. His prescient understanding of the importance of social media dramatically changed the concept of the traditional catwalk show, resulting in seasonal extravaganzas for Chanel that became the highlight of the fashion calendar as he consistently transported an invited and online audience to

# KARL LAGERFELD

**OPPOSITE:** Karl Lagerfeld accepts applause at Fendi, 2015.

**ABOVE:** Fluid femininity for Chloe, in the shape of casual, tie wrap top and loose-legged pants, 1973.

**RIGHT:** Re-inventing the classic Chanel codes, Lagerfeld included updated versions of the Little Black Dress in all his collections, Spring/Summer 1990.

increasingly spectacular theatrical presentations.

At the age of 17, Karl Otto Lagerfeldt accompanied his mother to see a Christian Dior show at the Palais Esplanade in Hamburg. For a young man obsessed with drawing and reading, the show made a big impression and soon after, he left Germany to finish his education in Paris, thinking fashion was a direction he would like to pursue. An opportunity came in 1954, when his winning design for a competition sponsored by the International Wool Secretariat (a brightly coloured coat with an interesting buckle neckline) secured him a job at the couture house of Pierre Balmain. His next move, working alongside Jean Patou for several years, cemented his education in the techniques of couture, but it also left him bored, convinced that the immediacy of youth-orientated ready-to-wear was where his future lay.

From the 1960s onwards, Lagerfeld's name (he had dropped the t in his surname when he started working professionally) was associated with numerous brands, including Chloé, Krizia, Valentino, Max Mara, Charles Jourdan, Fendi and Chanel, all of which thrived under

# KARL LAGERFELD

**OPPOSITE LEFT:** Longline jacket in oversized check tweed, with distressed chiffon trim on the pockets and sleeves from the Spring/Summer Haute Couture collection 1992.

**OPPOSITE RIGHT:** Original Chanel signatures, pearls, camellia, gilt buttons and rope chain belts all re-imagined for a younger clientele, for the 1992 Haute Couture show.

**BELOW:** As creative director at Fendi from 1965, Lagerfeld revamped the luxury fur market, by adding colour and creativity. Dressing gown style full length fur cut into decorative horizontal bands, 1997.

his artistic input. 'I hate to be bound to one thing,' he told *WWD*, and in addition to juggling multiple freelance contracts including knitwear, shoes and bags, he also launched a label under his own name.

In 1965, Lagerfeld began an association with the Italian house of Fendi, run by the five Fendi sisters in Rome. His idea to inject fun into fur started with his design of the now iconic inverted FF logo and the concept of subverting the traditional fur coat by introducing unusual pelts like squirrel and rabbit, adding vibrant colour and printed patterns. His radical ideas proved hugely successful for Fendi, resulting in a lifelong position as creative director. In Paris, his work for Chloé, a fashionable ready-to-wear label that gained cult status in the 1970s, brought further acclaim as he tapped into the nostalgia of the 1930s, presenting unrestrictive fluid pieces including bias-cut dresses and wide culotte pants, utilizing lively colourways and graphic prints.

It was his tenure at Chanel, however, from 1983 until 2019, that brought Lagerfeld unimagined fame and wealth. Charged with reinvigorating a house that had floundered for a dozen years, since the death of the indomitable Mademoiselle Chanel, he studied the archives and concluded 'irreverence' was the way forward. Taking the existing signature tropes of Chanel, Lagerfeld, a master stylist, tapped into the excess of the 1980s and injected wit and humour into every item. Inspired by all forms of popular culture and obsessively curious about the future, Lagerfeld spent the next three decades rebranding Chanel for a younger audience, deconstructing tweeds with LED lights, reimagining suit proportions with micro-mini hot pants, and making the brand sexy with fishnet bodysuits and supersized gilt chains. Lagerfeld presented his last collection for Chanel in March 2019.

# TOM FORD

**AUSTIN, TEXAS, USA** 1961–

**HIGHLIGHTS**
Peep-hole slinky evening dresses, low-slung pants, devoré kaftans.

**DESIGN ETHOS**
'Hedonism, luxury, glamour and sex, I've always been in love with all those things.'

WITH THE CHISELLED GOOD LOOKS OF A HOLLYWOOD MOVIE STAR, IT WAS INEVITABLE THAT TEXAN-BORN TOM FORD WOULD CAST HIMSELF IN THE ROLE OF HANDSOME LEADING MAN TO PROMOTE HIS NAMESAKE FASHION LABEL.

**BELOW:** Tom Ford, notable for his tenure at Gucci.

Having built his reputation revamping the Italian heritage brand Gucci into a multi-billion-dollar luxury label, Ford became fashion's poster boy for success based on the premise of overt sexuality, a theme he continued to exploit for his own alluring advertising campaigns.

Credited with turning around the ailing fortunes of the family-run leather, luggage and accessories business and relaunching it for a younger generation, Ford moved to Milan in 1990 to start designing Gucci's ready-to-wear womenswear under the auspices of Dawn Mello. Four years later, appointed as creative director, his remit had expanded to oversee the entire public face of the company in charge of the collections, the design of the stores, packaging, fragrances and all company advertising. Under Ford's unwavering vision of seductive hedonism, a label that was very much in decline when he took over suddenly became the hottest ticket in the Italian fashion calendar.

Ford's overarching approach to style owed much to the sophisticated glamour of Halston's 1970s New York disco. Ford was successfully selling the dream of a celebrity lifestyle, as much as the fluid jersey dresses that were needed to be a part of it. Global adulation arrived in 1995 with a catwalk collection that featured snake-hipped girls wearing low-slung velvet pants and royal blue satin shirts casually unbuttoned to the waist. When Madonna appeared at the MTV Video Music Awards that year in a replica outfit, looking like a real-life Barbie doll with blonde bouffant hairpiece, and told journalists she was wearing 'Gucci, Gucci, Gucci', the Tom Ford fan base exploded.

At 13 years old, Ford moved from Texas to Santa Fe, New Mexico, with early thoughts of a possible career working as an actor in Hollywood. A move to New York in his late teens saw him enrol at Parsons School of Design, where he studied architecture. His entrance into fashion began with designer Cathy Hardwick, working on Seventh Avenue in the rag trade district of New York; offering minimal

# TOM FORD

**ABOVE:** Mini kaftan dress with bell sleeves and plunging neckline, fastened with double G clip, made from swirling devoré velvet, 1995.

**ABOVE:** Low slung satin hipster pants, with bandeau bra top and feather boa, from the Spring/Summer Ready-to-Wear collection, 1995.

**TOP:** Actress Gwyneth Paltrow in red velvet trouser suit in 1996 at the MTV Video Music Awards in New York.

**OPPOSITE:** Slimline velvet pencil skirt with satin bow tie at the waist, with matching jacket with satin lapels, 2002.

**BELOW:** Madonna dressed entirely in Gucci, satin shirt, hipster pants and horse bit belt, at the MTV Awards 1995.

qualifications for the job, he relied on intelligence and charm instead, telling the proprietor Armani was his favourite designer because he recognized that she was wearing the label. There were also brief periods of work as design director for womenswear for Perry Ellis before he relocated to Milan and launched his debut collection for Gucci in 1994. It took a year to hit his stride, but Ford's transformation of Gucci into the most desirable label of the decade was underway. As an antidote to Seattle's anti-fashion grunge movement, Ford endorsed high-end luxury embedded with sex appeal. Celebrities were clamouring to be dressed in Gucci, with Gwyneth Paltrow memorably stylish in his red velvet trouser suit at the MTV Awards in 1996. Fabrics were lavish – leather, satin, devoré silk, velvet, fur – and he embraced abstract pattern, snakeskin, leopard skin and crystal embellishment.

The overall aesthetic unfailingly championed insouciant rock chic. Gucci models were lean and androgynous (as were many of his clothes); Stella Tennant and Amber Valletta were favourites, walking the runway with messed-up hair and smudged eyeliner. The advertising campaigns shot by Mario Testino endorsed this louche image, with a semi-naked Carmen Kass shown pulling down her pants to reveal a Gucci G shaved into her pubic hair; the ultimate controversial statement in an era of logo-led publicity.

In 2000, while still at Gucci, Ford took over as creative director in charge of the ready-to-wear collections at YSL Rive Gauche, plundering the archives to present his own take on Saint Laurent's iconic trouser suits. His own label, Tom Ford, was launched in 2005, first with fragrance and cosmetics, followed by men's and women's collections, all of which deviated little from the laid-back glamour that had already been so successful for their brand ambassador. In 2022, the business was sold to Estée Lauder for £2.2 billion.

# TOM FORD

# DOLCE & GABBANA

**DOMENICO DOLCE**
**POLIZZI GENEROSA, SICILY, ITALY** 1958–

**STEFANO GABBANA**
**MILAN, ITALY** 1962–

**HIGHLIGHTS**
Corsets, lace, luxury patchworks, religious iconography, leopard skin biker jackets.

**DESIGN ETHOS**
Modern reworking of the cultural aesthetics of the traditional Sicilian family.

FEW LABELS ARE AS INSTANTLY RECOGNIZABLE AS THE TONGUE-IN-CHEEK, SEX-BOMB DYNAMISM OF DOLCE & GABBANA (DOMENICO DOLCE AND STEFANO GABBANA).

Their modern interpretation of the Sicilian woman, confident, powerful and unbelievably sexy, has underpinned a decades-spanning success story that continually references the sartorial traditions of southern Italy. Dolce cites the founding concepts for their creativity as 'Sicily, tailoring and tradition' and these have not wavered since the launch of their debut collection in the mid-1980s. Pulsating with Mediterranean light and colour, their brand identity fuses tradition with fantasy, masculine with feminine, innocence with provocation.

Outstanding advertising campaigns pay homage to the sensual imagery of the Italian film industry, referencing the old-school allure of movie stars like Sophia Loren and Gina Lollobrigida in evocative imagery, conjuring up the glamour of *la dolce vita*.

Early collections were characterized by the adoption of exquisite corsetry as outerwear; the glimpse of a satin bra, its shape exaggerated by circular stitching, was designed to be seen under a skimpy cardigan; fitted satin shift dresses trimmed with lace that skimmed the female form were reminiscent of 1950s lingerie and temptress high heels. To offset the familiar tropes they have become known for, they also like to surprise, mixing different periods, baroque and hippy chic, juxtaposing contrasting textiles, animal

# DOLCE & GABBANA

**OPPOSITE:** Designers Stefano Gabbana (left) and Domenico Dolce on the catwalk in Milan, 2024.

**LEFT:** Feminine curves in classic corsetry with elasticated sides and lace up front as eveningwear from September, 2023.

**BELOW:** Crinoline-like cage skirt, worn over black leotard body with transparent chiffon overdress, shown for the Spring/Summer 2103 collection.

print and lace, and in 1994, abandoning the Sicilian aesthetics of floral full skirts and fringed shawls in favour of mafioso-inspired pinstripe suiting and men's cotton vests. Their association with Madonna, who personally chose the duo to create 1,500 costumes for her 1993 The Girlie Show tour, elevated their international fame and helped cement their status as Italy's most innovative design partnership.

The DNA of Dolce & Gabbana (usually referred to as D&G) comes from Sicily, where Domenico

Dolce grew up, and where his business partner (they are no longer romantically linked) Stefano Gabbana holidayed as a child. Sicilian-born Dolce came from a fashion background: he was introduced to making clothes as a seven-year-old, and later helped out in the shop of his family's small clothing business. Stefano Gabbana hails from Milan and trained in graphic design, working for a series of advertising agencies in the city while trying to move into fashion. When Gabbana applied for an assistant's job with Giorgio Correggiari, it was another assistant, Dolce, who picked up the phone; the two men met and were immediately drawn together through a shared love of Italy and a fantasy Italian style.

In the early 1980s they both worked as freelance designers, Gabbana concentrating more on accessories, and Dolce on clothes, gaining experience to launch the foundations of their own collaborative label. With just 2 million old Lire (about £1,000 today), D&G presented their first show, 'Real Women', in Milan fashion week in 1985. They made every outfit themselves and with insufficient funds to pay professional models, they used friends, who were asked to style the outfits with their own accessories. Despite their youth, their romantic vision of Italy was applauded and the label that celebrated Sicilian aesthetics gained traction season by season, slowly building to become an international brand that now includes menswear, childrenswear, accessories, underwear and perfume.

Working together for so many years, trusting their instincts and experience to make the right choices, has been a joint effort with all decisions shared. 'I am precise and hard-headed, while Stefano is more impulsive and extroverted,' Dolce has said. Together, they have succeeded in remaining independent, creating a flamboyant style that is timeless not trend-led, while continuously developing colour-infused collections stamped with D&G originality. In 2002, they designed all the costumes and accessories for Kylie Minogue's 'Fever' European tour, developing an ongoing friendship that led to further collaborations with their '*Piccola Principessa*' (Little Princess). Their glitz and glamour creativity is perfectly suited to the spectacular stage clothes needed to present Kylie's sell-out shows.

# DOLCE & GABBANA

**OPPOSITE:** Regal red in a collection of fine lace outfits, embellished with bugle beads and gemstones from 2014.

**RIGHT:** Hippy chic patchwork blouse, collaged from contrasting prints and vibrant colour palette, worn with long slimline skirt stitched from multiple strips of floral brocade, 2020.

# DAPPER DAN

| **EAST HARLEM, NEW YORK CITY, USA** 1944– |
|---|
| **HIGHLIGHTS** Invention of Logo-mania, balloon-sleeved, mink-lined bomber jacket. |
| **DESIGN ETHOS** 'More is always better.' |

**BELOW:** Dapper Dan in New York, 2019.

FETED AS A FASHION VISIONARY BY THE URBAN NEW YORK RAP ARTISTS HE CATERED FOR, DAPPER DAN SPENT DECADES FINE-TUNING AN AESTHETIC THAT MIXED HIGH-END CASUALWEAR WITH LUXURY BRANDING.

Credited with being the inventor of a street style genre that fed seamlessly into the 1980s hip hop movement, Dan's conspicuous 'Logo-mania', stamping multiple logos in a decorative style on to sweatpants, bomber jackets and beanie hats, became his recognized signature. His ideas of taking and reappropriating luxury brand logos was compared to similar practices of 'sampling' in the music of that era.

After years of legal lawsuits against him and fashion exile from an international industry that cultivates the exclusivity of trickle-down trends, Dan's unique creativity was finally acknowledged by many of the brands who once wanted to prosecute and shut him down. When Gucci's creative director Alessandro Michele visited Dan's Harlem home in 2017, he revealed that 'all the major fashion houses have Dapper Dan on their mood boards'. The Gucci x Dapper Dan collaboration that followed featured a 300-piece collection of '90s-inspired ready-to-wear clothes and accessories drawn from Dan's archives, rebooted with Italian finesse and the indomitable spirit of Harlem. Voted by *Time* magazine as one of the 100 Most Influential People of the Year in 2020 and referred to by *Vogue*'s contributing editor André Leon Talley as 'An iconic fashion hero to multiple generations, fusing street with high sartorial elegance', the legendary couturier continues to work from his home turf, inspired by the people around him.

Daniel Day was born at home in a tenement building in East Harlem, the fourth boy of seven children (the

DAPPER DAN

**ABOVE:** Overt logomania seen on hip hop band Salt-N-Pepa, in 1988.

**RIGHT:** The best role model for his own collections, Dapper Dan seen here in New York, 2023.

last three were girls) to what he remembers as a 'poor as hell' family. His father worked three jobs to support everyone, and as a child Dan learned quickly that if he wanted to have anything he would have to get it himself. Hustling to survive, he became proficient at gambling, earning thousands of dollars as a teenager, which allowed him to stop living in hand-me-downs. An elderly mentor on the street, impressed with his winning style, gave him the name Dapper Dan. Drugs offences led to a brief spell in prison, but also provided the impetus to turn his life around. Always a prolific reader, serious thinker and obsessive about the clothes he wore, Day took the idea of fashion and used it as a transformative means of power, to provide instant gratification by way of perception, for the people of his community.

Concentrating on luxury goods, the sort of 'swag' that gave people clout ('Black people on the rise wanted furs and diamonds'), he opened his first shop on 125th Street in Harlem in 1982, buying wholesale mink coats, marking prices up and selling on to a clientele of cash-rich hustlers, gangsters and kingpin drug dealers; the shop stayed open 24 hours a day for eight years to cater to their unconventional lifestyles. Day was responsible for the pivotal relationship between early '80s hip hop music and an obsession with high-end European brands. Recognizing that young people aspired to wear these labels, he took

# DAPPER DAN

himself first to the library to learn about the origins of the logo, and then studied fabric properties, how to use a sewing machine and leather printing techniques to create his own fabrics, featuring the recognizable iconography of Fendi, Gucci and Louis Vuitton. 'I never thought of it as a crime, it was not taking anything tangible,' he has said.

The unique style of urban luxury he created, embellishing logos all over expensive sweats and leather baseball-style jackets, became the 'must have' uniform for a street cred generation of athletes and rap artists, including Mike Tyson, Floyd Mayweather Jr., JMJ of Run-D.M.C., LL Cool J and Salt-N-Pepa. There were many legal wranglings about copyright infringements and in 1992, Day was forced to close down his boutique after Fendi took action and won. He continued working from home designing clothes for private customers. In 2017, when Gucci showed a bomber jacket with decorative fur strips and oversized balloon sleeves on the catwalk, social media exploded with cries of exploitation, on Day's behalf, resulting in the 2018 collaboration that paid homage to Day's 'Blackenized' aesthetic. 'Logo-mania is probably my biggest achievement in terms of fashion,' Day has said. He recently re-established a brand-new Dapper Dan atelier in Harlem, which offers bespoke garments, with exclusive fabrics specially printed by Gucci.

**ABOVE:** Designs go mainstream with a collaboration with Gap x The Brotherhood Sister Sol x Dapper Dan, 2023.

**RIGHT:** Gucci re-imagined by Dapper Dan for his 2018 partnership with the Italian luxury brand.

# JOHN GALLIANO

**GIBRALTAR, SPAIN** 1960–

**HIGHLIGHTS**
'Les Incroyables' graduation show, bias-cut slip dresses, signature newsprint crinoline.

**DESIGN ETHOS**
Fantasy-driven narratives of romance, forged from a magpie's instincts to skilfully collate a pastiche of historical influences.

WITH A STANDING OVATION AND RAPTUROUS APPLAUSE ECHOING AROUND JUBILEE HALL IN COVENT GARDEN, JOHN GALLIANO'S END-OF-YEAR GRADUATION SHOW IN 1984 IGNITED A SOARING TRAJECTORY OF IMAGINATIVE THEATRICALITY THAT HAS ALWAYS BEEN BASED ON EXTENSIVE HISTORICAL RESEARCH.

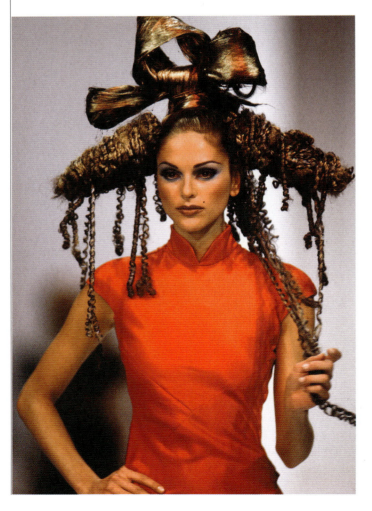

As a final-year fashion student at Saint Martin's School of Art in London, inspiration for his ground-breaking first collection, 'Les Incroyables', came from the rebellious spirit of the French Revolution, with the young designer paying meticulous attention to every minor detail. Fabrics were stained with tea then baked in the oven, coat linings were embellished, and Galliano asked his father to drill holes in oxidized pennies to make buttons. His entire student collection was bought by Joan Burstein and then displayed in the windows of her exceptional boutique Browns in South Molton Street.

Within a month of graduating, 24-year-old Galliano was in business, completing orders and worrying about his next collection from the front room of his parents' house in south London. His extraordinary talent for complex tailoring and brilliant fabric manipulation was recognized by the industry at large, and within a decade he had been asked to take over at Givenchy, the first British designer to head up a French couture house. Two years later, Bernard Arnault, CEO of LVMH, appointed him as creative director at Dior, the most prestigious of all the Parisian fashion houses, where within five years of his arrival profits had increased by over 50 per cent.

# JOHN GALLIANO

Born in Gibraltar but moving with his family at the age of six to south London, Juan Carlos Antonio Galliano was brought up in a strict Catholic family, where his father worked as a plumber and his flamenco-dancing mother earned money as a dinner lady. An accomplished illustrator, the shy adolescent gained a place on the renowned fashion course at Saint Martin's in 1980, where he was encouraged to study historical dress at the V&A museum, and also took a job as a dresser at the National Theatre. His forays into London clubland with a Soho crowd of

**OPPOSITE:** Inspired by global travel, Galliano re-works a traditional cheongsam dress, worn with magnificent headdress intertwined with plaited hair, from the Spring/Summer Ready-to-Wear collection 1993.

**ABOVE:** John Galliano with Kate Moss (left) in 1994.

177

innovators who all spent hours brainstorming wild 'costumes' to make their grand nightclub entrance (Boy George, Stephen Jones, Jeremy Healy) was the catalyst for Galliano's own reinvention, which would impact future creativity.

Through the Galliano fashion prism came elaborate transformation on an epic scale. He invented a fantastical backstory to every collection he produced, whether for his own label, Givenchy or Dior; decorative invitations that set the mood would be sent out to press and favoured clients. A rusty key, a scarlet ballet shoe or a cache of love letters provided clues to an intriguingly titled show ('Afghanistan Repudiates Western Ideals 1985'), suggesting complex narratives for the visual experience about to unfold. Models were encouraged to be characters, to play out their part; in his romantic 1986 'Fallen Angels' collection the girls had their hair doused in talcum powder and walked the catwalk scattering talc over the audience. For the finale, Galliano sprayed water over them, making their make-up run, and the thin Empire line gowns they wore stick sensuously to their bodies.

With his move to Paris and the backing of LVMH, Galliano's fashion fantasies became more spectacular; he successfully collaged multicultural influences with 20th-century iconography, skilfully creating new aesthetics that were always surprisingly beautiful. In 1996, Galliano spliced together Wallis Simpson and Pocahontas as inspiration for Dior; in 1989, he mixed the vivid colour palette of tribal Africa with London's

# JOHN GALLIANO

**OPPOSITE:** Imaginative storytelling, executed with superb tailoring and lavish embellishment defined Galliano's Haute Couture collections for Dior, from Spring/Summer 2007.

**RIGHT:** Sticking mostly to a black colour palette, Galliano has won a new legion of fans for his anti-fashion deconstructivism at Maison Margiela, 2020.

cockney pearly queen's wardrobe. 'I'm an adventurer, a storyteller, a dreamer,' he said in 2010 while discussing the creative process that he is so passionate about.

Galliano was dismissed from Dior in 2011, and his own label closed two years later. After a temporary residence with Oscar de la Renta in 2013, Galliano began a new chapter in his life with the conceptual Parisian house Maison Martin Margiela (MMM).

Since 2015, Galliano (as artistic director of the renamed Maison Margiela) has continued to weave his own brand of magical storytelling through collections that blend haute couture ideals with ready-to-wear realism, of sorts. The Galliano aesthetic for MM champions deconstructivism, disruptive tailoring and oversized styling and has ensured the Japanese split-toe tabi shoe has become a covetable cult signature.

179

# ALEXANDER McQUEEN

**LEWISHAM, SOUTH LONDON**
1969–2010

**HIGHLIGHTS**
Oyster shell and razor clam dresses, 'Armadillo' shoes, 'bumster' trousers, bias-cut tartan.

**DESIGN ETHOS**
Historical romance visually challenged with punk subversivity.

IN 2011, MORE THAN 600,000 PEOPLE BOUGHT TICKETS TO SEE THE APTLY NAMED 'SAVAGE BEAUTY' EXHIBITION AT THE METROPOLITAN MUSEUM OF ART IN NEW YORK CITY, AN EXTRAORDINARY RETROSPECTIVE OF THE LONDON DESIGNER ALEXANDER MCQUEEN.

**BELOW:** Lee Alexander McQueen in New York in the late 1990s.

His visionary approach to fashion, which had shocked and fascinated the world, was rooted in a deep understanding of the processes of haute couture, and the exemplary levels of craftsmanship achieved by the ateliers to create such artistry. The show celebrated McQueen's technical ingenuity, detailing the complex autobiographical narratives that underpinned his work, as every season he pushed boundaries and challenged conventional definitions of fashion and art. His theatrical runway presentations referenced visual clues from historical folklore, his Scottish ancestry, the transient beauty of the natural world and an obsessive curiosity about death and decay.

Through the intricacies of his cutting techniques, masterful manipulation of colour and innovative use of irregular materials (glass, feathers, leather, wood), McQueen's imaginative collections regularly questioned the perception of beauty within society. 'Savage Beauty' chronicled McQueen's story, from the cleverly distressed clothes of his Saint Martin's School of Art graduation show, to his masculine-style 'bumster' trousers, cut daringly low across the hips and shown in 1995, and the exotic digital prints and

**OPPOSITE:** Model Stella Tennant in sculptural white trouser suit from the Givenchy Couture collection, 1997.

ALEXANDER McQUEEN

iridescent enamel paillettes used to create original silhouettes for his 'Plato's Atlantis' collection in 2010.

The youngest of six children, Lee Alexander McQueen was brought up in the tough environment of the East End of London, his father working as a black cab driver and his mother a teacher and florist. At the age of 17, he started an apprenticeship at the Savile Row tailors Anderson & Sheppard and for two years he learned how to sew, pad undercollars, set a sleeve and make perfect buttonholes; it taught him the defining principles of English tailoring achieved through cut, proportion and colour. A brief spell as a pattern cutter with Japanese designer Koji Tatsuno based in Mayfair introduced him to the idea that fabric could be used in a three-dimensional way to create fantasy on the runway, and a job at Romeo Gigli in Rome presented concepts of feminine deconstructionism.

At 21, McQueen applied for a teaching position at Saint Martin's School of Art; Bobby Hillson, founder of the prestigious MA course, recognized his genius and instead immediately offered him a place to study for a master's degree, which was financed by a £4,000 loan from his favourite Auntie Renee. His legendary graduation show, 'Jack the Ripper Stalks His Victims', featured precision cutting: tight silk jackets with ruffled, gravity-defying peplums; a soft pink frock coat printed with barbed wire threads; and gathered calico skirts, torn, burned and covered randomly with red paint to denote blood. English eccentric

# ALEXANDER McQUEEN

**LEFT:** McQueen's gothic sensibility often presented ideas that challenged popular notions of beauty. Philip Treacy parasol hats with strapless applique dress with hooped skirt from the Autum/Winter Ready to Wear show, 2009.

**BELOW:** Erin O' Connor in fitted op art dress with matching boots and gravity-defying orange corsage on her shoulder, for Givenchy, 2000.

Isabella Blow, an associate editor at British *Vogue*, was so impressed with McQueen's show that she bought the entire collection and became a tireless supporter, muse and mentor.

McQueen began to establish a reputation as the bad boy of English fashion, his early originality provoking outrage as he presented models wearing transparent 'cling film' minidresses splattered with red mud that resembled blood, sheer tops cut so short that they revealed the model's genitalia and 'bumster' trousers that exposed bare buttocks. 'I know I'm provocative. You don't have to like it, but you do have to acknowledge it,' he said. In 1996, he was named British Designer of the Year, and in October he was appointed as the creative director of the House of Givenchy. The alliance was not a happy one, with McQueen creatively constrained by the aristocratic Parisian establishment that, he said, did not support his vision. His first collection was deemed underwhelming by the press, and McQueen infuriated LVMH's Bernard Arnault by agreeing that he too thought the collection was 'crap'.

In 2001, McQueen departed Givenchy and signed a deal with Tom Ford's Gucci group, who would gain a majority stake in his namesake label, helping to turn him into a global brand with menswear, womenswear, perfume launches and stand-alone retail premises. McQueen continued to present showstopper catwalk collections that skilfully explored themes of masculine tailoring with dazzling touches of feminine beauty; in 'Widows of Culloden' in 2006, Kate Moss appeared as a hologram in a glass pyramid above the stage, swathed in fluttering ruffles; 'Plato's Atlantis' in 2010, which revealed seaweed hairdos and exaggerated 'Armadillo' shoes, was one of the first fashion shows to be streamed live. In 2010, nine days after his mother's death, Alexander McQueen took his own life.

# MIUCCIA PRADA

**MILAN, ITALY**
1949–

**HIGHLIGHTS**
Black nylon backpack, industrial uniforms, ugly shoes, high-waisted pencil skirts.

**DESIGN ETHOS**
Unconventional aesthetics that disturb societal norms of beauty and sexuality.

MIUCCIA PRADA, ALWAYS RESPECFULLY REFERRED TO AS 'MRS PRADA' BY JOURNALISTS, IS A FASHION DISRUPTOR WHO HAS BUILT A GLOBAL LUXURY BRAND ON THE PREMISE OF 'UGLY CHIC' INFORMED BY ORIGINAL THINKING.

**BELOW:** Miuccia Prada at the Council of Fashion Designers of America awards in 2004.

Her hybrid aesthetic, which blends strange print combinations and unusual colours in unpredictable style combinations has become a Prada signature, along with the subtle silver metal triangle that signifies fashion 'insider'. At a time in the mid-1990s when high-end fashion hit the pinnacle of explosive glamour, Prada was exploring abstract concepts that leaned heavily on minimalism, creating a visual DNA for the brand that ultimately resulted in changing the way people viewed luxury.

Mrs Prada has consistently challenged the customer to embrace sartorial bad taste and invert preconceived values; her fashion empire launched on the success of a waterproof, military grade black nylon Vela backpack she presented in 1984. A factory produced a very specific type of nylon for her that was more expensive than silk because the thread was super thin, and although she says 'at the beginning everybody hated everything I did', within a season the nylon bags had become cult items.

Disregarding historical conventions, Prada spontaneously clashes random ideas to create something highly original that challenges the eye; her concepts inevitably copied by other designers the following season. Early collections in retro shades of 1970s sludge upholstery prints resembled suits befitting studious librarians, and she has endorsed ankle socks with high heels and sandals, collaborated with Damian Hirst on a plexiglass handbag that mixed real beetles

# MIUCCIA PRADA

**ABOVE:** Quirky individualism seen in this sleeveless silk dress with appliqued parrot motif from Spring/Summer 2005.

**RIGHT:** Longline quilted parka with double opening zip detail and oversized pockets designed for Miu Miu, Autumn/Winter 2013.

and bugs with embroidered ones, and audaciously embellished classic tweeds with fox fur and ostrich feathers. The younger, slightly cheaper diffusion line she oversees, Miu Miu (taken from Miuccia's childhood nickname), was added in 1992, offering an even more contradictory mix of unorthodox constructs, which has proved equally influential.

After studying at the University of Milan for a PhD in political science, Miuccia Prada spent time at the Piccolo Teatro, where she took mime lessons in order to find the 'unknown' and the 'new'. She was a member of Italy's Communist Party and is said to have dressed in Yves Saint Laurent to distribute leaflets. In the mid-1970s she inherited the Fratelli Prada company, her grandfather's successful leather goods business that he founded in 1913, selling high-quality luggage and shoes. Her love of fashion was inherently personal – she always wants to look different from everybody else so she dressed in second-hand clothes, utilitarian uniforms bought from trades outfitters and things she had made herself. Not really liking anything she saw in fashion, she entered the family business in 1978 to shake things up a bit and 'to search for the absolute opposite of what was already out there'.

Her first innovation, the range of simple nylon bags that questioned the parameters of luxury, led to a ready-to-wear collection that was presented in Milan in 1988. Railing against banality in fashion, her imaginative ethos has always been to search for something different, something that disturbs the equilibrium and offers a fresh perspective. She coined the phrase 'ugly chic' to describe her style.

Working in partnership for the last 45 years or so with Patrizio Bertelli, her down-to-earth Tuscan businessman-husband, has catapulted the family business into a global fashion empire that continues to push experimental boundaries. As a fashion maverick, she has stuck unsympathetic shades of brown and purple together, updated deceptively simple school uniform-type dresses, played with 1950s-style cartoon illustrations, and created quirky banana earrings; her ability to unfailingly astonish the customer is the only consistency that can be relied on. Shunning the idea that she is an artist, Prada has become renowned for her philanthropic projects, has her own foundation and gallery space in Milan designed by architect Rem Koolhaas, and frequently commissions new-wave directors to produce content for Miu Miu. In 2020, Prada asked Raf Simons to join as co-creative director of her label – an alliance that has allowed a merging of intellectual minds to create thoughtful fashion.

**LEFT:** Fitted coat made from taupe lace from the Autumn/Winter collection, 2008.

**OPPOSITE:** Green paper yarn dress with scattered tulip prints from the Spring/Summer collection, 2023.

MIUCCIA PRADA

# DRIES VAN NOTEN

| ANTWERP, BELGIUM 1958– |
|---|
| **HIGHLIGHTS** Decorative tunics over slim trousers, lavishly embroidered tailoring. |
| **DESIGN ETHOS** Understated elegance that balances beauty and functionality, creating playful choices through colour and print. |

AS ONE OF THE FAMOUS 'ANTWERP SIX' DESIGNERS WHO HELPED ESTABLISH BELGIUM AS A VIABLE FASHION FORCE IN THE EARLY 1990S, DRIES VAN NOTEN IS KNOWN FOR HIS STUNNING COLLECTIONS THAT FUSE COLOUR, PRINT AND TEXTURE IN CONTEMPORARY WEARABLE PIECES THAT ARE DECEPTIVELY LOW-KEY BUT NEVER DULL.

His recognized signature endorses continual evolution of multicultural styles that brilliantly juxtapose different influences. 'I like to play with contrasts,' he has said. Soft fluidity is created through complex layering of different fabrics, classical shapes are embellished with sophisticated embroidery, and colours and motifs are subtly reworked, cleverly shifting depth of tone and scale, so that every outfit shines individually.

Founded on artistic principles of beauty, Van Noten has always rejected the notion of celebrity-led, dictatorial trends in favour of a refined style achieved through his unique way of working. Unlike most designers who present themed collections, Van Noten

**LEFT:** Dries Van Noten on the catwalk in Paris, 2023.

**OPPOSITE LEFT:** Applauded for his wearable shapes made up in spectacular fabrics. Heavily embellished jacket with fur collar worn over chiffon shirt and multicoloured cropped pants, 2008.

**OPPOSITE RIGHT:** Loose shirt with elongated rhombus print, worn over diaphanous skirt with matching scaled down prints, from the Autumn/Winter show 2017.

# DRIES VAN NOTEN

prefers to work on each piece as a standalone item. The desirable clothes that have become his trademark consistently surprise his multigenerational clientele and are created with the intention of longevity. 'When I design a collection, I want to create options. The last thing I really want to do is say how people have to dress,' he told the *New York Times*.

As a designer who operates outside the giant conglomerate fashion system, Van Noten has proved incrementally over a 30-plus-year career that his blurred masculine/feminine aesthetic is universally coveted by clients who choose clothes to express their own personality. Having picked up many international fashion awards since his menswear debut in Paris in 1991, he was championed as *WWD*'s 2023 Designer of the Year, for both his men's and women's collections.

Immersed into the fashion industry from an early age, Dries Van Noten's grandfather worked as a tailor, and his father owned Belgium's most innovative retailer, which stocked the European prêt-à-porter collections. Van Noten remembers being taken to Paris, Milan and Dusseldorf to accompany his parents on buying trips and was encouraged to go into the family retail business, but instead followed his passion to train as a designer. He studied in the Fashion Design department at the Royal Academy of Fine Arts in Antwerp, freelancing as a commercial designer to support his studies, and after graduating in 1981 he set up his own company, specializing in menswear.

In March 1986, a group of college friends hired a van and set off across Europe to showcase their avant-garde clothes at London Fashion Week, where they were collectively dubbed the 'Antwerp Six' (their individual names were considered too difficult to pronounce). Van Noten sold a small collection of shirts to Barneys New York and Whistles in London, with a request that he should produce some smaller sizes for women. His first retail boutique opened in his home town in 1986, and to this day Van Noten runs his business from a warehouse loft in the Antwerp docks, considering it 'a healthy distance from any big fashion city'. He debuted a menswear collection in Paris in 1991, his distinctive womenswear, which now generates bigger sales, arriving in 1993. The two collections totally inform each other in terms of colour, print and shape, Van Noten's creative process barely changing from season to season. It is not art, but the challenge of producing something beautiful but also commercially successful that pushes him to create opulent outfits that electrify the runway. Every aspect of the exuberant, saturated colour palette and detailed embroidery (designed in Antwerp but hand-produced by around 2,000 workers in remote villages around Kolkata in India) is carefully considered, to ensure the pieces are wearable but maintain a touch of bohemian imperfection. 'For me perfect beauty is boring, that's my starting point,' he explains.

Since 2018, Van Noten has been backed by the Spanish company Puig, which has allowed him greater expansion, opening several stores in China and a gallery space in Los Angeles. In 2017, he was appointed a baron by King Philippe of Belgium in recognition of his contribution to the cultural life of his country.

**RIGHT:** Showcasing his love of vibrant colour, at the finale of the Autumn/Winter Ready-to-Wear collections in Paris in 2008.

# DRIES VAN NOTEN

# MARC JACOBS

**NEW YORK, AMERICA** 1963–

**HIGHLIGHTS**
Grunge collection for Perry Ellis 1992/93, 'Mouse' ballet pumps, Louis Vuitton collaborations with artists Stephen Sprouse, Takashi Murakami and Yayoi Kusama.

**DESIGN ETHOS**
Familiarity of classic design upended with a cool urban twist.

AS A REACTION TO THE FORMULAIC POWER DRESSING THAT PREVAILED IN THE 1980S, FASHION EXPERIENCED A HUGE ANTI-FASHION MOVEMENT IN THE EARLY '90S THAT WAS BEST EXEMPLIFIED BY MARC JACOBS' INFAMOUS 'GRUNGE' COLLECTION FOR PERRY ELLIS IN 1992.

BELOW: Marc Jacobs on the runway in New York, 2014.

As a talented young Parsons graduate, his appointment in 1989 as head of women's design at the classic sportswear label had been newsworthy only for the fact that he was a 25-year-old prodigy who had previously been awarded Design Student of the Year at the prestigious New York fashion school.

Sensing the cultural signs of change within fashion by taking his cues from the music and street styles of Seattle, while recognizing the emergence of a new sense of beauty achieved through imperfection (waif-like Kate Moss challenges the flawless glamour of Cindy Crawford), Jacobs presented his rebellious Spring/Summer 1993 show, telling the *New York Times*, 'That's the way beautiful girls look today, a little bit unconcerned about fashion.' The spirit of Seattle's thrift-store staples, Dr Marten boots, knitted beanie hats and messy hair were all reimagined through the intuitive vision of Jacobs. Plaid lumberjack shirts produced in luxury washed silks were tied casually around the waist, striped tees and long john leggings were reinterpreted in the finest cashmere, and trashy floral dresses (the sort Kurt Cobain was fond of) were made from delicate floaty chiffon. Fashion critics were impressed – *WWD* called him the 'Guru of Grunge' – but buyers rejected the concept of selling high-end pieces that resembled 'cheap fashion'. Production was stopped and six months later Jacobs was fired for

# MARC JACOBS

**RIGHT:** At Louis Vuitton, Jacobs became the most influential designer of his generation, injecting the staid leather brand with a desirable, understated luxe, as here in this form fitting leather coat, with Peter Pan collar, large patch pockets and textural buttons, from 2010.

creating what turned out to be a seminal collection with long-term influence. With the ending of one career, Jacobs moved on to become one of the most successful designers in contemporary fashion, with a namesake brand and a 16-year tenure as creative director at Louis Vuitton.

Marc Jacobs was born in New York and after graduating from the High School of Art and Design, he attended Parsons School of Design in Greenwich Village to study womenswear. He was brought up by his fashion-conscious grandmother, a talented knitter who hand-knitted three oversized, brightly coloured op art sweaters for his final year collection, which caught the attention of Robert Duffy, an American businessman. Duffy secured Jacobs' first post-college employment with a Seventh Avenue company called Sketchbook, and the two men quickly became professional partners, launching the label Marc Jacobs and showing his first collection in 1986. Continually applauded by the fashion industry, Jacobs was the youngest designer ever to win the highest honour of a Council of Fashion Designers of America (CFDA) award in 1987 and has gone on to win a record-breaking nine times in his career.

His reputation as an important voice in fashion brought him to the attention of the LVMH group, who offered him the position of artistic director at Louis Vuitton, and also bought a majority shareholding in

# MARC JACOBS

**LEFT:** Sixties style influences for Louis Vuitton, Summer 2013. Slimline mini shifts, boxy jackets, crop tops and long fluid dresses in graphic checkerboard prints, modelled by pairs of twins travelling down four full-size working escalators.

**BELOW:** Jumping off a full-size Louis Vuitton steam train complete with leather luggage, the Autumn/Winter 2012 presentation harked back to a glamorous age of style. Lavish fur collars embellished boxy jackets, over dresses that flared gently to the ankle, decorated with jewelled buttons and tall plumed hats.

Marc Jacobs International, providing the financial support he needed to expand his own line. His remit at Louis Vuitton when he arrived in 1997 was to inject the rather staid luxury leather company with some savvy streetwise credibility through the creation of the house's first high-end ready-to-wear collections. His remarkable success in helping to reposition the brand as a global fashion powerhouse was unprecedented; the catwalk shows he presented were rich in colour and texture, inspired by such diverse ideas as the golden age of travel, the kinky fetish-themed movie *The Night Porter* (1974), and Parisian showgirls. His collaborations with artists Takashi Murakami, Stephen Sprouse and Yayoi Kusama, who daubed cute cartoon characters, neon graffiti and multicoloured spots over the traditional handbag range, helped boost profits from millions to billions.

After 16 years as creative director, Jacobs stepped down from Louis Vuitton in 2013 to concentrate on his own product lines. He has retail shops around the world selling heavily branded casualwear and accessories, his Heaven by Marc Jacobs range focuses on youthful subcultures, and his catwalk shows continue to surprise the audience, such as his crediting of the programme notes for Autumn/Winter 2023 to ChatGPT.

# IRIS VAN HERPEN

**WAMEL, NETHERLANDS**
1984–

**HIGHLIGHTS**
Laser-cut skeleton dress, leather corset belts, crystallization dress of splashed water.

**DESIGN ETHOS**
Exploring boundaries of new technology to create couture fashion as an art form.

A RECENT EXHIBITION IN PARIS AT THE MUSÉE DES ARTS DÉCORATIFS PAID TRIBUTE TO THE PIONEERING CREATIVITY OF DUTCH-BORN DESIGNER IRIS VAN HERPEN.

'Sculpting the Senses' examined the complex work of an 'artist' whose sculptural take on fashion challenges existing notions of haute couture. Van Herpen's thought-provoking creations ignite conversations about the limitations and purpose of fashion, specifically couture, and her contribution to rethinking the definition of luxury in the 21st century should not be overlooked. Clearly inspired by living forms found in the natural environment and fascinated with architecture, Van Herpen's aesthetic explores the possibilities of fluidity, extending the space around a woman's body, using perpetual movement to create modernistic and multidimensional shapes. Much of her sensory output presents a visual dichotomy that can be hard to pin down; consisting of strong shapes and soft materials, undulating natural forms and jutting structural rigidity, her work celebrates fragility and plays with scale, transforming tiny organic matter into dazzling red carpet creations.

All of these visual signatures underpin the extraordinary diversity of a designer who rejects conventional clothing in favour of something more esoteric. A vocal advocate for the adoption of technical development in fashion, her collaborations with digital technology companies provides expertise in 3D printing, laser-cutting and 3D moulding – all essential elements of her process. Van Herpen's quest to invent new ways of making showstopping couture

**LEFT:** Elris Van Herpen with Chinese actress Fan Bingbing at the Autumn/Winter show, 2024.

**ABOVE:** Astonishing visual beauty achieved by technical innovation with modern materials and old-fashioned techniques of craftsmanship, on the catwalk in Paris, 2020.

# IRIS VAN HERPEN

pieces does not, however, negate the importance of the traditional artisan. 'My atelier is focused on craftmanship, which is directly linked to innovation. There's some futurism in what I do, but I'm really into old, forgotten craft techniques, which I then combine with new materials and techniques,' she says.

Her skill in fusing the traditional with the experimental has resulted in extraordinarily memorable stage outfits for musicians Beyoncé, Lady Gaga and long-time fan Bjork, known for her unconventional sartorial choices. Recognized internationally as one of the most radical designers of her generation, Van Herpen's magical pieces transcend the intersection between fashion and art.

As a child growing up in the Netherlands, Van Herpen's first introduction to fashion was playing in her grandmother's attic, where she found a 'mini museum' of old garments that opened her eyes to a different era of dressing. She played the violin and liked painting, but it was dancing that captivated her, and she trained for many years in classical ballet, with a future as a professional dancer in mind. A fascination with movement of the body and a realization that clothes can be transformative led instead to a career

**BELOW:** The 3-D printed polyamide skeleton dress from the *Capriole* collection created by flexible hinges is assembled on to the model's body, from Autumn/Winter 2011.

**OPPOSITE:** Blurring the boundaries of fashion and high art with fabric manipulation that evokes beauty from the natural world, from the Spring/Summer Haute Couture show, 2020.

in fashion, and she graduated with a degree in Fashion Design at Arnhem's ArtEZ Institute of the Arts in 2006. There were brief periods of work with Alexander McQueen in London and with the Dutch artist Claudy Jongstra, before Van Herpen set up on her own, launching her label in 2007.

Based in Paris, Van Herpen quickly established herself as a unique vision in a competitive field, developing a futuristic style of high-tech couture that often makes descriptive analysis impossible, her dance background instrumental in her expressive manipulation of the way clothing relates to a moving body. Without drawing any designs on paper, each piece is determined by the properties of the material she is experimenting with, with no idea of what the final outcome will be. 'It is quite a chaotic process, but I do think that's where unexpected things come from,' she says.

Van Herpen's reinvention of ethereal femininity is dependent on collaboration with others, who help develop unimaginable materials with diverse qualities not usually associated with clothing. The Autumn/Winter 2011 'Capriole' collection featured her stylized 'Skeleton' dress, now held at the Costume Institute in New York. Made in conjunction with the digital technology company Materialise, the rigid structure was constructed using a 3D printing process called selective laser sintering that builds layers of nylon powder into a computer-generated shape, refined by sanding and coating once the structure has cooled. The complexities of such innovations (the illusion of dresses made from 'water' using crystalline formations) are time-consuming, so the collections she presents twice a year at the exclusive Paris Haute Couture Week are limited to around 20 pieces. Unsurprisingly, her beautiful work is viewed by many as art, and has become a permanent fixture in museums around the world.

IRIS VAN HERPEN

# PHOEBE PHILO

**PARIS, FRANCE**
1973–

**HIGHLIGHTS**
Military tailoring, Birkenstock-type sandals with mink lining, alphabet necklace.

**DESIGN ETHOS**
Modern classicism defined by perfect proportions and luxury fabrics.

## FOLLOWING IN THE TRADITION OF COCO CHANEL, THE DESIGNER PHOEBE PHILO IS A WOMAN WHO VERY MUCH DESIGNS WITH HERSELF IN MIND.

'I've always had a sense that if I can't wear it, what's the point?' she has said. Her straightforward, minimalist approach to fashion has earned her a legion of devoted fans, collectively dubbed the 'Philophiles', who wait eagerly for her next 'drop' and cannot imagine dressing without the perfectly proportioned staples Philo has presented over the last 20 years or so. As a cool Londoner, self-assured but totally unassuming, Philo makes a thoughtful figurehead for the fuss-free elegance she has become synonymous with. Her innate style quirks – tucking her hair into the top of a roll neck sweater, wearing wide-leg pants that skim the soles of her white Stan Smith trainers – are cool-girl tics, immediately plagiarized by every copy-cat wannabe.

First reviving the style credentials of cult 1970s label Chloé, and then later at the French house of Celine, Philo's fresh versions of practical modernism are a recurring aesthetic; essential pieces you didn't know you needed until she provided them. Committed to a neutral colour palette of grey, navy, khaki, taupe and ivory, her beautifully cut coats, fluid silk pants and oversized cotton shirts are always refined but understated. She creates desirable, luxurious clothes that have captivated a generation of real women, fed up with the concept of statement trends, all inevitably redundant by the following season. Philo's influence on the wider fashion landscape has been immense; her focus on sophisticated wearability makes the

**ABOVE:** Backstage with her models, Phoebe Philo in Paris, 2004.

# PHOEBE PHILO

self-indulgent eccentricities of other designers look woefully outdated, and tellingly everything she does is immediately copied at both ends of the retail spectrum.

Although she was born in Paris, Phoebe Philo's family had moved back to north London by the time she was two. The eldest of three children who came from an artistic background, she spent her teenage years customizing clothes on her sewing machine and later studied for a fashion degree at Central Saint Martins. On graduating, she worked closely alongside her art school friend Stella McCartney, who had been made creative director at Chloé in 1997, taking over from Karl Lagerfeld. Philo succeeded McCartney in 2002, turning the label into one of the coolest brands in Paris.

Playing with the established feminine/masculine ethos of the brand (created by Gaby Aghion in 1952),

she is credited with bringing a boho 'It' girl party vibe to Chloé, undercut with street-smart urban energy; exemplified by her pin-tucked baby doll tunic dresses, casual boyish pants and clumpy clogs. The large 'Paddington' bag she introduced in 2005, made from soft 'worn-in' leather and loaded with an industrial-sized metal padlock, became an instant modern classic, still much coveted by in-the-know Philo fans.

After stepping down from Chloé in 2006 for more time with her family, it was announced in 2008 by Bernard Arnault, CEO of the LVMH group, that Philo was to return to fashion as the creative director of Celine. Founded in 1945 by Céline Vipiana originally as a children's leather footwear company, Philo felt the lack of design heritage would work in her favour: 'Celine was a clean slate,' she has said. Her tenure at the French house cemented her credentials as a force in fashion, and she was acclaimed for her collections that celebrated real women, consistently providing them with extremely wearable grown-up clothes (high-waisted silk trousers with a contrasting side stripe, Crombie coats with satin lapels) constructed in beautiful fabrics that were made to last.

After almost a decade of unrivalled financial and

# PHOEBE PHILO

critical success at the helm of Celine, Philo departed in 2017 amid much speculation about her future direction. Rumours of a comeback, her own label backed by a minority LVMH stake, finally came to fruition in October 2023 with a limited range of seasonless pieces that can only be found online. The launch confirmed that Philo's signature style remains intact: blouson leather jackets, restyled army combat fatigues, oversized cardigans and a range of immaculately cut coats and trouser suits, all beautifully cut pieces imbued with design longevity.

**OPPOSITE:** A predominantly black and white colour palette used to create a feminine aesthetic from 2005.

**RIGHT:** Unstructured tailoring for Celine, 2011.

**FAR RIGHT:** Early collections for Chloe sealed Philo's reputation for casual elegance with a playful edge. Model Hana Soukupova wears silk camisole over a cotton T-shirt, Autumn/Winter 2004.

# RICHARD QUINN

**LEWISHAM, SOUTH LONDON**
1990–

**HIGHLIGHTS**
Exaggerated balloon coats, latex opera gloves, leopard print puffball skirts, floral face masks, outsize botanical prints.

**DESIGN ETHOS**
Old-school couture silhouettes infused with intense colour and dynamic prints.

FASHION HISTORY WAS MADE IN 2018 WHEN QUEEN ELIZABETH II WAS GUEST OF HONOUR AT DESIGNER RICHARD QUINN'S AUTUMN/WINTER CATWALK SHOW IN LONDON.

Photos of the event were splashed around the world; it was the Queen's first, and only, appearance on the front row, and the wider public seemed curious to know who exactly was Richard Quinn? Having only recently graduated from his MA at Central Saint Martins, he had quickly established a recognizable aesthetic that fused the craftsmanship and shapes of grand couture with extravagant prints and the occasional subversive sex dungeon trope. Intentionally designed to shock, he calls the dramatic vision he creates 'cracked couture'.

The inaugural Queen Elizabeth II Award for British Design presented by Her Majesty, to recognize an up-and-coming designer with outstanding talent who has a consideration for social responsibility, pushed Quinn's burgeoning career sky high overnight. With the Queen perched centre stage on her own cushion, Quinn showcased a collection that featured neon

**LEFT:** Richard Quinn, supported by Billy Porter and stylist Sam Ratelle, backstage in 2019.

**ABOVE LEFT:** Floral motorbike helmet and thigh high polka dot boots on the catwalk for Queen Elizabeth II in 2018.

**ABOVE RIGHT:** Extreme silhouette with exaggerated statement sleeves and oversized bow at waist from the Autumn Ready-to-Wear show, 2019.

# RICHARD QUINN

bright motorcycle helmets, swishy foil-like dresses and floral latex leggings. The designer paid homage to the monarch's signature head scarf by creating handkerchief dresses made up entirely from heavily patterned mismatched silk scarves.

Within months, Amal Clooney had visited his studio (underneath a railway arch in Peckham) to be fitted for a bespoke dress for the Met Ball. Her standout red carpet outfit, designed to interpret the theme 'Heavenly Bodies: Fashion and the Catholic Imagination', stole the show. Over a fitted corset and satin cigarette pants, Clooney wore a floor-length sweeping train printed with roses and lilies chosen by Clooney for their religious connotations, the whole thing fabricated from a silver foil-type fabric to replicate a stained-glass window effect.

As the youngest of five children, Richard Quinn came from a fiercely loyal family in south-east

**LEFT:** Daisy print swing coat with matching headscarf, face mask and tights, 2019.

**OPPOSITE:** Oversized duster coat with full blown sleeves and collar made from floral print, silver foil fabric for Autumn/Winter 2018.

London. His father ran a scaffolding company and Quinn has said he 'grew up in his lorry, with no idea you could make a living from art'. A perceptive teacher at Chislehurst and Sidcup Grammar School suggested he apply to Central Saint Martins and after completing a foundation course, he gained work experience in fashion, interning for tailor Richard James, and designers Christopher Shannon and Michael van der Ham. Quinn went back to art school to study for a BA and subsequently an MA, spending most of his time in the college print rooms, where he developed a love for vibrant colour and wild pattern. His graduation show in March 2016 evidenced many of the fledgling ideas he has since developed into recognizable signatures; playing with scale, he joyfully mixed giant florals with smaller complementary prints, contrasted blooming garden scenes with his love of black-and-white houndstooth check, and pushed 1950s-style puffball silhouettes to dramatic proportions, contrasting tough vinyl textures with soft tulle and dressing models in gingham gimp masks. This outstanding student collection helped Quinn's meteoric rise, winning the H&M Design Award in 2017 and the £44,000 cash prize that came with it, allowed him to set up his business studios with high-tech digital printers, which can be accessed by other luxury brands, independent designers and students looking to print sample pieces.

# RICHARD QUINN

Following on from the global exposure generated by the endorsement of the royal award, Quinn has quietly evolved his reputation as a designer who keeps pushing boundaries without losing sight of his objectives. His 2020 collaboration with Moncler, the luxury Italian fashion house best known for its high-end sports clothes, saw their first couture offering with Quinn's giant daisy print turned into a hard-to-miss voluminous puffer jacket that fused functionality with fashion. A recent move from the Peckham railway arches he started out in to larger premises has not derailed Quinn's direction, and he produces couture-level pieces (akin to Christian Lacroix) that can be translated into ready-to-wear clothes. His Spring/Summer 2024 collection, dedicated to his beloved father and shown in one of London's grandest, flower-filled hotel ballrooms, provided old-style elegance: an abundance of embellishment, intricate embroidery, balloon-sleeved opera coats and ultra-feminine dresses with stiff cupola-shaped skirts, all infused with Quinn's intense love of colour and opulence.

# RESOURCES

## BOOKS

Bacque, R, *Kaiser Karl: The Life of Karl Lagerfeld*, Woodbridge: ACC Art Books, 2020.

Banks-Blaney, William, *25 Dresses: Iconic Moments in Twentieth-Century Fashion*, Quadrille, 2015.

Baudoit, Francois, *A Century of Fashion*, Thames & Hudson, 1999.

Blum, Dilys E, *Shocking! The Art & Fashion of Elsa Schiaparelli*, Yale University Press, 2003.

Bluttal, Steven, and Mears, Patricia, ed., *Halston*, Phaidon Press Ltd, 2001.

Breward, Christopher, Gilbert, David and Lister, Jenny, ed., *Swinging Sixties*, V&A Publications, 2006.

Burstein, Joan, *Browns: Forty Years of Fashion*, Browns Ltd, 2010.

Casadio, Mariuccia, *Moschino*, Thames & Hudson, 1997.

Chenoune, Farid, *Jean Paul Gaultier: Fashion Memoir*, Thames & Hudson, 1996.

Day, Daniel R, *Dapper Dan: Made in Harlem: A Memoir*, Random House, 2019.

De La Haye, Amy and Tobin, Shelley, *Chanel, The Couturiere at Work*, V&A Publications, 1994.

Fabbri, Fabriano, *The Event Horizon, Fashion Styles from the Sixties to Today*, Atlante, 2013.

Homer, Karen, *Little Book of Dior, The*, Welbeck, 2020.

Howell, Georgina, *In Vogue, Six Decades of Fashion*, Penguin Books Ltd, 1975.

Jones, Terry and Rushton, Susie, *Fashion Now*, Taschen 2006.

Jouve, Marie-Andrée, *Balenciaga*, Assouline, 2004.

Mackenzie, Mairi, *...isms Understanding Fashion*, Herbert Press, an imprint of A&C Black Publishers, 2009.

Mendes, Valerie and De La Haye, Amy, *20th Century Fashion*, Thames & Hudson, 1999.

Mendes, Valerie, *Pierre Cardin: Past, Present, Future*, Dirk Nishen Publishing, 1990.

Montana, Claude and Cro, Marielle, *Montana*, Thames & Hudson, 2011.

O' Hara Callan, Georgina, *Fashion and Fashion Designers*, Thames & Hudson, 1998.

Palomo-Lovinski, Noel, *The World's Most Influential Fashion Designers: Hidden Connections and Lasting Legacies of Fashion's Iconic Creators*, BES Publishing, 2010.

Reed, Paula, *Fifty Fashion Looks that Changed the 1980s*, Conran Octopus, 2013.

Sozanni, Franca, *Dolce & Gabbana*, Assouline, 1999.

Steele, Valerie, *Fashion Designers A–Z*, Taschen, 2023

Thomas, Dana, *Gods and Kings, The Rise and Fall of Alexander McQueen and John Galliano*, Penguin, 2015.

Watt, Judith, *Ossie Clark 1965–74*, V & A Publications, 2003.

Watson, Linda *20th Century Fashion*, Carlton Books, 2003.

## WEB RESOURCES

anothermag.com
businessoffashion.com
cnn.com
guardian.com
i-d.vice.com
lofficiel.com
nytimes.com
observer.com
telegraph.co.uk
theface.com
thelovemagazine.co.uk
thetimes.co.uk
vanityfair.com
vogue.com
wmagazine.com
wwd.com

# PICTURE CREDITS

**Alamy Stock Photo**: Abaca Press 87, 171, 178, 185R; Album 13R; Art World 33; Associated Press 73L, 175, 189L, 191, 202; Chronicle 70; DPA Picture Alliance 139, 198; Everett Collection Inc 138B; Granger – Historical Picture Archive 79; Grzegorz Czapski 111; Imago 195; PA Images 63, 96, 207; Pacific Press Media Production Corp. 126; Penta Springs Limited 22R; Pictorial Press Ltd 51L; Retro AdArchives 133B; Sipa US 179, 187; Stephen Chung 31; Trinity Mirror/Mirrorpix 7, 165L; Zuma Press Inc 39L.

**Duffy** © Duffy Archive 65T

**Emma Baxter-Wright:** 64

**Getty Images:** Aitor Rosas Sune/WWD/Penske Media 206; Antonio de Moraes Barros Filho/Wirelmage 189R, 193; Apic 29L; Art Streiber/Penske Media 101; Art Streiber/WWD/Penske Media 154, 156; Bertrand Guay/AFP 127L; Bettmann 53L, 53R, 57, 59, 76, 133T; Bill Brandt 41; Chicago History Museum 13L, 17L, 24, 26L, 26R, 35, 43L, 43R, 46; Christophe Simon/AFP 186; Claude James / INA 70; Culture Club/Bridgeman 30R; d' Ora/ullstein bild 23; Daily Mirror/Mirrorpix 117T; Daniel Simon/Gamma-Rapho 71, 107L, 159, 176; Dave Benett/Getty Images 116, 157R; David Corio/Redferns 117B; Dimitrios Kambouris 172; Dimitrios Kambouris for Marc Jacobs 192; Dominique Maître/WWD/Penske Media 38, 203R; Donato Sardella/Penske Media 138T; Edward Wong/South China Morning Post 66T; Emanuele Sardella/Penske Media 97; Emmanuel Dunand/AFP 196; Eric Robert/Sygma/Sygma 106; Evening Standard/Hulton Archive 32; Fairchild Archive/Penske Media 56, 80, 84, 92, 94, 108, 110, 124, 153; Fairchild Archive/WWD/Penske Media 85L; Fine Art Images/Heritage Images 30L; Francois Guillot/AFP 155, 203L; Gareth Cattermole 122, 123L; Genevieve Naylor/Corbis 54, 55; George Chinsee/Penske Media 95; George Chinsee/WWD/Penske Media 109L, 109R, 134, 135; Gie Knaeps 129R; Giorgio Lotti /Mondadori Portfolio 69; Giovanni Giannoni/Penske Media 89, 142, 143, 145, 146, 129L; Giovanni Giannoni/WWD/Penske Media 151, 162L, 205R; Gregory Pace/FilmMagic 184; Guy Marineau/Penske Media 82T, 82B, 130; Guy Marineau/WWD/Penske Media 125; Harlingue/Roger Viollet 15; Hulton Archive 51R; Hulton-Deutsch Collection/Corbis 65B; Indianapolis Museum of Art 102; Jean-Pierre Muller/AFP 39R; Jeff Kravitz/FilmMagic, Inc 166T; Jeremy Bembaron/Sygma/Sygma 112; Jerry Cooke/Corbis 25; Joe Maher 44; John Chillingworth 47; John van Hasselt/Sygma 88, 177; Jon Furniss 120; Jon Levy/AFP 158; Joy Malone 173R, 174; Kevin Mazur Archive/Wirelmage 166B; Keystone 45, 68; Keystone-France/Gamma-Keystone 21; Keystone-France/Gamma-Rapho 34, 50; Kirstin Sinclair 98; Liz Hafalia/The San Francisco Chronicle 119; Michael Ochs Archives 173L; Michel Arnaud/Corbis 162R; Michel Dufour/Wirelmage 201; Michel Maurou/WWD/Penske Media 128; P L Gould/Images 118, 157L; Pascal Le Segretain 182; Penske Media 103; Peter White 123R, 127R; Picture Post/Hulton Archive 48; Pierre Schermann/WWD/Penske Media 77B; Pierre Vauthey/Sygma 83, 85R, 131, 140, 141, 149; Pierre Verdy, Jean-Pierre Muller/AFP 74; Pierre Verdy/AFP 67, 147, 167, 183, 185L; Reg Lancaster/Daily Express 73R; Reginald Gray/WWD/Penske Media 78, 81, 161L; Roberta Bayley/Redferns 93; Roger Viollet 14, 17R; Ron Galella, Ltd./Ron Galella Collection 100, 148; Santiago Felipe 204; Sarah Morris 114; Sasha 36; Saviko/Gamma-Rapho 91; Sepia Times/Universal Images Group 19; Stephane Cardinale/Corbis 86, 194; Stephane de Sakutin/AFP 150; Susan Wood 61T; Terry Fincher/Express/Hulton Archive 72; Terry Fincher/Keystone 42; Thierry Chesnot 188; Thierry Orban/Sygma 99; Thomas Iannaccone/WWD/Penske Media 132, 180; Tom Johnson/WWD/Penske Media 164; ullstein bild 37; Venturelli for Fendi 160; Venturelli/Wirelmage 169R, 170; Victor Virgile/Gamma-Rapho 75, 104, 105, 107R, 152, 161R, 163, 165R, 169L, 181, 197, 199; Vittoriano Rastelli/Corbis 136; Vittorio Zunino Celotto 168; WWD Photo/Fairchild Archive/Penske Media 121; WWD/Penske Media 205L; Yoshikazu Tsuno/AFP 113

**Jim Lee Photography:** 61B

**Kerry Taylor Auctions:** 60, 62, 90

**Metropolitan Museum of Art:** 9L, 9R, 10T, 10B, 11

**Public domain:** 8, 12, 16, 18, 20, 22L, 28, 29R, 40, 52

**Scala:** The Metropolitan Museum of Art/Art Resource/Scala, Florence 27

**Shutterstock Editorial:** Nat Farbman/The LIFE Picture Collection 49

**Wikipedia Commons:** 77T